PRAISE FROM THE EXPERTS FOR *THE TOP TEN MISTAKES* . . .

"Selling is an art, a science and a game. Todd Duncan's book, *The Top Ten Mistakes Salespeople Make and How to Avoid Them*, gives you valuable strategies to creatively fine-tune your sales performance and win the game more often by learning what *not* to do!"

—TOM HOPKINS,
The Builder of Sales Champions,
Author of *How to Master the Art of Selling*

"Todd Duncan has the unique ability to turn defeat into victory. In *The Top Ten Mistakes Salespeople Make and How to Avoid Them* he reveals how to transform your career and personal life by confronting specific mindsets and habits that limit your potential. By applying Todd's strategies, you'll take your profession to the next level."

—JOHN C. MAXWELL,
Founder, The INJOY Group

"This powerful, practical book will show you how to plough through the obstacles to sales success and turbo-charge your sales career."

—BRIAN TRACY,
Brian Tracy International

"Why learn from your own mistakes when you can learn from others'? Todd Duncan's book, *The Top Ten Mistakes Salespeople Make and How to Avoid Them*, helps sales professionals eliminate the mental blocks and change patterns of action that are keeping them from succeeding. As usual, Todd takes his real-world experience in directions that can turn careers around 180 degrees."

—ANDY ANDREWS,
Author of the *New York Times* Bestseller, *The Traveler's Gift*

D0594673

"Todd Duncan's latest book, *The Top Ten Mistakes Salespeople Make and How to Avoid Them*, is a real-world look at why sales professionals fail and what it takes to succeed. I wish I had read it at the beginning of my sales career. If I had, I would have sold more and had more fun."

—MARK SANBORN, PRESIDENT,
Sanborn & Associates, Inc.,
Author of *The Fred Factor: How to Make Every Moment Extraordinary*

"Todd Duncan is the master sales trainer. *The Top Ten Mistakes Salespeople Make and How to Avoid Them* outlines the sabotage thinking that prevents most of us from reaching our potential and shows us how to conquer it. The book is incredibly valuable for anyone selling anything."

—BOB KRIEGEL PH.D.
Author of *How to Succeed in Business Without Working so Damn Hard!* and *If It Ain't Broke...BREAK IT!*

"This book is a powerful 'wake-up call' for the salesperson who can't figure out why more customers aren't buying from him or her. It's also a valuable, cautionary guide for the alert sales professional who wants to avoid these fatal mistakes."

—DANNY COX,
Author of *Leadership When the Heat's On*

"Todd Duncan's *The Top Ten Mistakes Salespeople Make and How to Avoid Them* is loaded with 'nuggets of wisdom' that every salesperson should know. It's brilliant and destined to become a sales classic!"

—MAC ANDERSON,
Founder, Successories

"This is a must read for anyone serious about their career in successful selling. *The Top Ten Mistakes Salespeople Make and How to Avoid Them* not only helps avoid crucial errors; it enables you to take your mistakes and turn them into winning relationships. A very powerful tool!"

— BARRY HABIB,
Contributing Editor, CNBC

Words of praise for Todd Duncan from just a few of the thousands who have experienced unprecedented sales success and transformed lives...

"It's hard to express the gratitude for the impact you have had on my life professionally and personally. You have shown me how to take my business and my life to the next level time and time again."

—LINDA,
Scottsdale, Arizona

"I have read your book and am experiencing the best time of my life! Everything in my sales efforts exploded. My family is happy, my friends enjoy my free time, and this week I was unknowingly asked in the sales meeting to tell the rest of the sales team what and how I am doing this! I FEEL GREAT!"

—LEON,
South Africa

"Thank you for challenging my future...for opening up my mind to what I can achieve. *High Trust Selling* has changed my life."

—MARILYN,
Langhorne, Pennsylvania

"Mr. Duncan, I bought your book and I've got to tell you that I could not put it down. It was really helpful to me. I am a dentist with a highly successful dental practice and your book has really helped me see my business goals in the context of my patients' values and needs."

—VIRGINIA,
Mt. Pleasant, South Carolina

"I just wanted to let you know, Todd, that you are simply the very best! *High Trust Selling* is a book that I am highly recommending to hundreds of people in my organization."

—KEVIN,
Atlanta, Georgia

"Todd, thanks to the High Trust Selling Academy, I finally have it all. A business that is thriving, a happy family life, a steady flow of business, a sense of where I want to go in my life, and a plan that will take me there. Thank you."

—PATRICK,
Oak Lawn, Illinois

"I have made a commitment to myself. A commitment so strong that as I type these words the 'goose bumps' are causing the hair to stand up on my arms. I can't find any other words to explain the commitment I have. Todd, this is all because of you and I thank you again for following your dreams."

—BRIAN,
Englewood, Colorado

"I have read your books and put to use what you talk about for both my personal and professional life. Things have never been better and I just wanted to say thank you. I just had to let you know what an inspiration you have been in my personal, spiritual, and professional life."

—DAVID,
Naperville, IL

THE TOP TEN MISTAKES
SALESPEOPLE MAKE
& HOW TO AVOID THEM

TODD M. DUNCAN

NELSON BUSINESS
A Division of Thomas Nelson Publishers
Since 1798

www.thomasnelson.com

Copyright © 2004 by Todd M. Duncan

All rights reserved. No portion of this book may be reproduced, stored in a retrieval system, or transmitted in any form or by any means—electronic, mechanical, photocopy, recording, or other—except for brief quotations in printed reviews, without the prior permission of the publisher.

Published in Nashville, Tennessee, by Thomas Nelson, Inc.

Nelson Business books may be purchased in bulk for educational, business, fundraising, or sales promotional use. For information, please email SpecialMarkets@ThomasNelson.com.

Previously published as *Killing the Sale: The 10 Fatal Mistakes Salespeople Make and How You Can Avoid Them*

Library of Congress Cataloging-in-Publication Data

Duncan, Todd, 1957–
   The top ten mistakes salespeople make and how to avoid them / Todd M. Duncan.
      p. cm.
   Rev. ed. of: Killing the sale / Todd M. Duncan. 2004.
   Includes bibliographical references.
   ISBN-13: 978-0-7852-8780-3 (trade paper)
   ISBN-10: 0-7852-8780-9 (trade paper)
   1. Selling—Handbooks, manuals, etc. I. Duncan, Todd, 1957– Killing the sale. II. Title.
HF5438.25D866 2007
658.85—dc22   2006036712

Printed in the United States of America
07 08 09 10 11 RRD 5 4 3 2 1

To all the excellent salespeople who
have shared with me the mistakes they
have made and how they now avoid them.
Thanks for making this book possible.

And to all the great people who want to
be successful salespeople—may your lessons be
learned in these pages and not in the midst
of your next sale.

Contents

Introduction

According to the World Federation of Direct Selling Associations, there are approximately 45.6 million sales professionals in the world today. And of that number, 12.2 million sell their wares in the United States. That means more than one-quarter of all the selling professionals in the world live here in our own backyard—in your city and mine, next door, down the street, and just around the corner. But let's put into perspective just how many salespeople that really is.

The Census Bureau reports that there are approximately 291 million people currently residing in the U.S. Are you doing the math? What that amounts to is that in the United States, incredibly, 1 in every 23 people is a salesperson. Mind you, that's not just 1 in every 23 working adults. That's 1 in every 23 people living in the United States—young and old, babies, children, teens, adults, and retirees. In other words, salespeople are literally *everywhere* you look. In your neighborhood, at the mall, in the movie theater, at your favorite restaurant, and at the gas station. On the bus, in your taxi, at your church . . . and in your mirror. And salespeople are selling everything imaginable. Stocks, bonds, homes, loans, copiers, and clothing. Cotton candy, peanuts, and ice-cold Coca-Cola. The latest technology. The greatest tip. The loudest stereo and the lightest phone. The funniest book and the fastest burger. Jobs, Jaguars, and fancy jets. In fact, the U.S. Patent and Trademark Office has granted more than 3 million patents in its history.[1] And what do you suppose happens to all those creations? The vast majority are sold—by you and by me.

We understand, like every other twenty-third person, that opportunity abounds in the sales profession. Of the $80 billion produced in sales in the worldwide economy every year, more than $25 billion is produced in the United States.[2] That's a lot of available commission. And some salespeople are making a killing. But a much greater percentage end up victims of the sales industry—and I'm not talking about the customers. I'm talking about the large percentage of salespeople who live paycheck to paycheck—those who go from job to job in search of that ever-elusive cakewalk to success. I'm talking about the large number of salespeople who quit the sales profession every year . . . thinking that it was their bosses' or coworkers' or customers' fault—when most often the truth is that it was no one's fault but their own.

Despite the promise of hope that the sales profession offers, many salespeople are left haggard and hopeless at the end of their workweeks. And many aren't achieving the success they set out for when they began. Sure, you could blame it on an oversaturated industry, but that's not really the problem. The real rub is that salespeople make mistakes. And lots of them.

Mistakes are inevitable in every profession, but especially the sales profession. I know because I've made many of them. Once I failed to send some very important paperwork to a client on time—despite her explicit instructions. My client was very frustrated when she called to let me know of my blunder. Yet instead of owning up to my mistake and apologizing, I became defensive. When she expressed her disappointment and threatened to take her business elsewhere, I told her I didn't care. Go ahead, I said. But five days later, I had lost not only her business but also the business of four other clients who had heard about the incident. Big mistake.

The fact is that when one person is involved in any endeavor, human error will eventually come into play. Mistakes *will* be made. We're not flawless individuals. But the sales profession, to the chagrin of some, is not an individualistic enterprise. Others are always involved. And if one person alone can botch a solo endeavor, a couple of people can absolutely ruin a shared enterprise. That's because all it really takes to produce some good ol'-fashioned mayhem are two strong-willed individuals with varying values and motives trying to force an agreement on something. And truth be told, that describes far too many selling efforts. Certainly some of mine, and I bet some of yours too.

The bottom line is that the sales industry can be a breeding ground for blunders: fallible salespeople offering fallible products to fallible customers. If we were all good at what we did and every customer was perpetually satisfied, there would be no need for this book. But unfortunately that's not the case. Salespeople still mess up. Customers still walk out. They still hang up. They still blurt obscenities—God forbid, but they do. And why? Because we're not always doing our job right. Because we sales professionals make mistakes. And some are bigger than others.

If every salesperson in the world made only three mistakes a year, that would be a whopping 136 million mistakes per annum. Of course, that's just hypothetical. Oh, that we could be so lucky to err so infrequently. The truth of the matter is that the vast majority of salespeople make more than three mistakes per year. A lot more.

Some of the mistakes we make are just normal bumps in the road to successful selling. Bruises to the ego. And often they can add some comic relief to our days. Like the general sales manager who was running late for an early sales meeting and subsequently took his shirt straight from the dryer and slipped it on in darkness. He made the meeting on time, and he certainly made a lasting impression. But not the impression he had intended. When he took off his jacket, several snickering salespeople let him know that his wife's lace panties were stuck to his back.[3] Ah, that dreaded static cling.

Other mistakes are more damaging. And like a sprained ankle or a broken arm, they can take time to mend. Like the young car salesman who misquoted the price of a new car to his former high-school principal. When the principal came back two days later to buy the car at the quoted price, the salesman had since recalculated the price with his boss and discovered an error. But the principal wouldn't budge. He still wanted the dealership to honor the original quote— mistake or not. And when the salesperson told the principal that he could not sell the car for a loss, the principal asserted, "Your math is to blame." To that, the salesman snapped back, "What do you expect from one of your former students?" And the rest of the story is history—along with the sale.[4]

Then there are fatal mistakes. Those errors in perception, practice, or performance that can kill not only a sale, but also a sales career. Like a blood clot, a bleeding ulcer, or a clogged artery, such mistakes will eventually put an end to your sales life if you do not tend to them. In April 2003 we were privy to an example of one such mistake at the corporate level when it was revealed that Delta Airlines' CEO Leo Mullins was willingly receiving a $12.2 million pay package for 2002 amid thousands of layoffs and additional requests (from Mullins himself) that other Delta employees take cuts in pay. And while the consequences are yet immeasurable, the news undoubtedly cast a luminous shadow over Delta's reputation as a respectable airline during a time when airline ticket sales were suffering considerably. As Delta and Mullins will certainly learn, it is such mistakes—fatal mistakes—that every sales professional must avoid like the plague. That's because the wounds of some sales mistakes just won't heal. They will kill your sales efforts; if repeated, they can kill your sales life.

And so, what is a sales professional to do? How can a salesperson like you, like me, steer clear of such lethal lapses in judgment? Well, that's what this book is all about. Based on thousands of interviews, years of research, and two decades of personal sales experience (and though I hate to admit it . . . making many of the mistakes), this book is specifically designed to help you steer clear of the fatal selling mistakes that can literally turn your selling career into a sales graveyard. I'm confident that if you follow the forthcoming strategies to avoid the 10 fatal mistakes that are discussed in this book, you *will* succeed in the sales profession, regardless of your product, service, or industry. And you won't just succeed now and then. If you create selling habits that allow you to consistently sidestep the fatal mistakes, you will succeed on a regular basis. And I'm not just talking about making more money. If you're ready, let me show you all that I'm talking about.

CHAPTER ONE

Mistake #1: Hyping

*Relying on "You can do it" propaganda to
maintain your sales motivation*

Take a look in the backseat of the average salesperson's car and you'll often find a bona fide smorgasbord of motivational merchandise. Books, tapes, videos, and pamphlets dedicated to the art and science of becoming more successful. Salespeople are known for building extensive libraries of pump-you-up products. And in the right context, there is certainly value in such merchandise. But the problem is that despite filling their heads with the time-tested wisdom of the sales sages and productivity gurus, many salespeople still find themselves in the middle of the pack, achieving only mediocre success. Maybe you've been there . . .

After attending your fourth sales and success event and spending more than $2,000 on products over the course of two years, you've found yourself whirling in a wind of debt without much success to show for it. You thought you made the investments that were necessary to take your selling success to the top, but it's beginning to look as if your investments are turning sour—and as a result, so is your attitude about selling.

After reading another book or listening to a new cassette or attending another seminar, you feel on top of the world. You feel confident that you can become the best salesperson in your field.

You're inspired to persevere when you read or hear phrases such as, "Success might be one call away!" So you keep trying—but things don't improve that much. You've tried to talk yourself into being a better salesperson. "I am a successful salesperson," you've reminded yourself. "Just keep plugging away. No pain, no gain," you've re-assured yourself. You've remained optimistic: "People want to buy my product! I *will* make a sale today!" But that approach works only for a couple of weeks. And so here you are, reading about a problem that you share with many other salespeople. Highs, then lows. Mountaintops and deep valleys. And you're probably wondering how this book is going to be any different from all the others you've read. Well, it won't be any different . . . until you understand the essence of one of the biggest mistakes salespeople make. That mistake is something I call "hyping."

WHAT'S ALL THE HYPE ABOUT?

Hyping, in the most basic terms, is relying solely on external stimuli—success books, cassettes, videos, seminars, and the like—to gain energy and maintain enthusiasm to sell. It's the equivalent of eating a Baby Ruth candy bar to sustain your energy for an entire week. It usually works in the short term, while the sugar is running through your veins, but it never lasts. Before long, you're back to where you started: tired, hungry, and in need of energy. And the same is true in the sales profession. The only difference in the world of sales is that the "Baby Ruths" are bound, audible, and often come with a name badge and a ticket.

Don't get me wrong here; success merchandise isn't the problem. The root of hyping lies in the false belief that any form of external stimulation can alone truly sustain your motivation to sell successfully. It simply can't and won't. Like sugar in your veins, it may give you a little pick-me-up for a short period of time, but before long you'll be left to fend for yourself.

IT ALL STARTS WITH A MOTIVE

Listen in on any criminal trial and you'll most likely hear one word repeated more than any other. In the widely publicized criminal trial of O. J. Simpson, this particular word was mentioned 226 times in the opening and closing arguments alone. "What's the word?" you ask. *Motive.*

"The defendant had a motive to commit the crime," argues the prosecution again and again. "The defendant did not have a motive to commit the crime," claims the defense over and over. And both the prosecution and the defense have good reason for their reiteration. Motive is ultimately the foundation of every criminal trial in America. The police detain a suspect on suspicion of motive. The state arraigns a suspect on probability of motive. And the court tries a defendant on legitimacy of motive. Why is all this talk about motive so significant? Because motive is at the heart of any action— good or bad. *Because motive leads to action.*

In the end, the fate of a defendant on trial usually lies in each lawyer's ability to prove or disprove that the individual's motives can be linked to a specific action. If the evidence shows that the individual's motives and the criminal act are an unlikely association, there is little ground to convict. *In other words, actions without motives are very unlikely to occur.* And the same is true of your actions as a salesperson.

Tapped Motives ⟶ Sustained Action

In the sales profession, you can't ignore your core motive for selling, then rely solely on hype to sustain your enthusiasm to sell. When you do, your enthusiasm will simply be based on emotional highs and lows, on how you feel that day or in that particular moment. And that will make it very difficult to sustain momentum. Trying to sustain your selling energy without tapping into your core motive for selling is like trying to run a marathon on inspiration alone—without food or water. No matter how much adrenaline you have as the starting pistol sounds, when your body is depleted of nutrients, no amount of inspiration will give your muscles the energy they need to keep going. And eventually you'll collapse.

Untapped Motives   ⟶   Unsustainable Action, or Hyping

As a salesperson, your level of enthusiasm depends heavily on your core motives for selling. That's because *motive* truly gives birth to action. External stimulation (books, tapes, seminars, and so forth) is supposed to be a catalyst that taps into your existing motives for the purpose of initiating consistent, motive-centered action. But external stimulation alone is not the true mother of action. And as a result, it will never sustain your enthusiasm in the long term. Maybe you can relate.

UNCOVERING YOUR TRUE MOTIVES

The bottom line is that true, sustainable enthusiasm in sales begins when you understand your core motives for selling. Unfortunately that's where too many salespeople go wrong. Either they don't understand their core selling motives, or they mistake money and

4

materialism for motives. And those mistakes lead to an emotional roller coaster of a career while they leave discerning customers with a bad taste in their mouths.

Have you ever thought about what might happen if your customers could hear everything you were thinking during a sales transaction? Would they still want to do business with you? Would they put their trust in you? Or would they walk away even sooner? If anything would reveal your current motives for selling (whether legitimate or not), letting your customers hear your thoughts surely would. For some salespeople, that would certainly be a good thing. It would show customers that their intentions are honest and mutually beneficial. But for many salespeople, revealing their thoughts would get ugly. It might sound something like this:

Salesperson:	Can I help you with something?
Customer:	No thanks. I'm just looking.
Salesperson:	Well, just so you know, we have a big sale going on right now on several of our new models . . . *Not really, but I'm telling you that because I want you to think you're getting a better deal than you really are.*
Customer:	Okay. I'll keep that in mind.
Salesperson:	Was there a particular car you were interested in? *Preferably one of our most expensive models so that I can get a big commission.*
Customer:	Well, I'm thinking about buying my daughter an Altima for her high-school graduation gift. But I'm not sure yet.
Salesperson:	Those are good cars. I used to own one myself before I traded it in for a Maxima . . . *The truth is that I've never owned either car, but I am telling*

you that so that I'll have more credibility with you when I talk you into spending your money.

Customer: I think a Maxima may be more than I want to spend right now.

Salesperson: Well, let me tell you that once I realized what I was missing, it was a no-brainer to spend a little more money to get the added safety and features that a Maxima offers. And ironically, now my daughter drives that car and loves it . . . *Actually I don't have a daughter, but telling you that helps me relate to you better and should help me talk you into buying the more expensive car, which means more money for me.*

Customer: What do you drive now?

Salesperson: *I was hoping you'd ask* . . . I just picked up one of our new 350Zs. Talk about a great car! *And if I can, I'll try to talk you into buying that one because that's the biggest commission I can make. The truth is that I don't own that car either, but it will—I hope—make you think I'm more successful than I really am.*

Customer: Those are great-looking cars. All right, I'm just gonna keep looking, and I'll let you know if I need anything.

Salesperson: No problem. Take your time. Why don't I go ahead and run some numbers on the Altima while you're looking? That way, if you find something you like, we're one step ahead of the game and you won't have to spend all day here. *And while I'm at it, I'll run numbers for the Maxima and 350Z, too,*

> *so that I can try to convince you to buy one of*
> *them. In fact, I'll make it look like you can get a*
> *great deal on the more expensive cars so that the*
> *Altima doesn't look like your best option.*

Customer: Okay.

Salesperson: Great. I'll be right back . . . *Get your checkbook*
ready.

Now, I know that's only a humorous example, but many customers would hear something similar if every salesperson's motives were audible. And that's sad. In fact, the fundamental source of hyping is that the "default" motives for many sales professionals are money, status, and job title. The problem is that those are merely rewards for successful selling—but they can never be core reasons to sell. They are results of successful selling, but not the roots. And such motives are certainly not earnest enough to keep you consistently motivated.

If you've been relying on something similar to keep yourself enthusiastic about selling—if you've been constantly reminding yourself of the potential payoff in order to get through tough times—if you've been solely looking to pump-you-up products to get yourself excited about selling, without looking at why you sell in the first place—then you're guilty of hyping. And you need to make a change before it's too late, before the "sugar high" wears off and you feel more lethargic about selling than when you started.

In order to break free from a hyping habit, you must leverage your core motives for selling. You must look deep inside yourself and answer the question of *why*: *Why, above every other reason, do I want to succeed in sales?* And if your answer is something that can be measured externally (for example, money, position, status), you will continually have trouble remaining motivated to sell—especially when difficulties arise. That's because *how* you sell (your action) is linked to *why* you sell (your motive), whether you know it or not.

We all have one predominant reason for why we sell. You have one motivating factor that dictates much of *how, when, where,* and *why* you go about your business of selling. And ideally *that* core motive drives you to new heights as a professional. But if you don't know your core motive for selling or are mistaken about its identity, you will constantly find it difficult to remain enthusiastic to sell. And when the going gets tough, you will have difficulty doing your job each day. *You will have the hope to sell successfully, but not the heart.* And like many, you will eventually call it quits, whether by force or by surrender.

The *breeding* ground for hyping is created when you don't take the time to understand the primary reason for why you sell. But the *proving* ground for hyping is cultivated when you try to pull up your proverbial bootstraps by looking externally for inspiration instead of internally where your true motivating factors exist. I found this out early on in my sales career . . .

There I was again, in the midst of another success seminar. Along with thousands of people in the auditorium, I was standing on my feet, beating my chest, and proclaiming, "I am great. I am a winner!" The energy in the room was as intense as the speaker himself. He had literally put the audience in a trance that made us feel invincible. With a booming voice he summoned us to "dream big dreams!" Again and again, he shouted, "You can overcome anything!" And I was truly believing it.

I vividly remember the speaker as he towered over his audience and told his rags-to-riches story. It would have been difficult to convince anyone there that he or she couldn't make something big happen. With eight hours of pure exhilaration in my veins and several hundred dollars' worth of resources at my side, I felt "programmed" for success. I was invincible. But as I would soon find out, that wasn't enough.

As the days passed, I felt my motivation waning. All the hype that external stimulation had summoned was beginning to dissolve, and reality was setting in. After a few weeks, my success tapes sought hibernation in the backseat of my car. And before much longer, I had only distant memories of the selling energy I had come to possess that day at the seminar. While I was contemplating this reality, I stumbled upon what is now the governing axiom in my life. I finally realized that motivation can't come from the outside. It must begin on the inside if it is to be sustained consistently.

PUTTING YOURSELF INTO THE EQUATION

Our company's average client spends approximately $5,000 each year on products and events in order to become a better, more enthusiastic salesperson. And of all the salespeople I speak to each year, nearly one-third of them have heard me speak before. These statistics indicate that salespeople want to be successful. They want to remain motivated. They're not just spending money on products and seminars because it's fun. They're in it to win. They're looking for something to keep them on par with their colleagues, and they're looking for the key ingredient that will keep them enthusiastic about selling in good times and bad—the magic potion that will keep them motivated to ascend and go beyond the hill of mediocrity. But many salespeople don't realize that the heart of remaining passionate about selling resides within them, not in the latest, greatest "how to" merchandise. It's simple: *when your core motives for selling are clear, your path to success is also clear.* And there's no other way around.

> It's simple: when your core motives for selling
> are clear, your path to success is also clear.
> And there's no other way around.

I am a motivational speaker. It's what I do for a living. So it's obviously in my interest to motivate people, right? But in all my years of speaking professionally, I've learned one thing about the advice and enthusiasm my products and seminars offer: they're not the keys for remaining motivated to sell successfully. I can be the most motivational person in the world. I can play the loudest, most inspiring music at my events. I can show you the most touching, moving film clips on five big screens that surround the room. I can have you walk on hot coals. I can fill your head with the most cutting-edge selling techniques and tactics. I can bring in the most successful salespeople on the planet to assure you that "you, too, can be successful!" and "you, too, can have everything you want!" But unless you understand your core motives for selling, everything I do will leave you full of short-lived hype. And eventually you will need another fix to keep you going—something or someone else to pump you up again.

The truth is that the only way to sustain selling enthusiasm is to first get clear on your motives, your underlying purpose for wanting to sell well.[1] That's why at my multiple-day events I reserve at least four hours of the first day for the attendees to do some real soul-searching—something many of them haven't done in years, if ever. I make them leave their briefcases, cell phones, pagers, and agendas at the event site, and I load them on a bus headed for the beach or a park or the mountains. Then I leave them there with one requirement: think. Think about what is most important to you in life.

10

Think about why you became a sales professional in the first place: Is that related to what's most important to you in life? Think about why you're still a sales professional today. Think about why you want to succeed in the sales profession. Think about why you are excited to meet with a new customer and win that customer's trust. Think about where you want to be one year, five years, and twenty years from now. *Think about your motives for living and for selling and doing both well.* I want them to think about such things because within their answers are the true keys to gaining and maintaining enthusiasm throughout a selling career.

EXPOSING YOUR INTERNAL MOTIVES

Recently my family and I spent a long weekend at our mountain home in Mammoth Lakes, California. For me it was a time to think, a time to reevaluate my life, my company, and my career as a sales trainer. It was a time to take a look at where I've been, where I am now, and where I desire to be days, months, and years down the road. It was *my* bus trip to the mountains to think. And during that time, I followed a simple thought pattern that I believe will help you secure and leverage your core motives for becoming successful in sales.

If you truly have a heart for the sales profession, the following exercise will help you do away with hyping once and for all, and it will provide you with the resources you need to remain enthusiastic about getting out of bed each day for work. It will help reveal the keys within you that are required for maintaining your energy to sell and sell well. So if you're ready, turn off your cell phone and pager or whatever else might distract you, and hop on the bus with me. It's time to do some real thinking.

What I am about to share with you is incredibly personal. These are my own results from completing an exercise, introduced to me by my friend and client Dan Trinidad, called "Ahead to 80." The objective of the exercise is to imagine and describe your life—past and present—as if you were eighty years old. But I want you to understand that as I share my results with you as a template for your own thoughts, the things that are important to me might not be important to you, and that is okay. You simply need to complete this exercise according to what's on *your* heart.

TODD DUNCAN . . . AHEAD TO 80

At the completion of my "Ahead to 80," exercise, I am forty-five years old. But remember, I am imagining myself at eighty years old, looking back on my life and describing in first person what I know and see. As you read over my thoughts, begin to jot down your own, in the margin, in your journal, or on a sheet of scratch paper. And if you've been struggling with hyping in your sales career, set aside some uninterrupted time this week to finish your thoughts.

Where do I live? My wife and I have been blessed to spend forty-five years of our lives a short walk from the crystal-blue waters of the Pacific Ocean in the city of La Jolla, California. Now, during our twilight years, Sheryl and I continue to stroll the boutique-strewn sidewalks and sunny sands of La Jolla where the water is blue, the air is clean, and the waves crash down just as they did that first day in 1989 when we wiggled our toes with excitement at the prospect of living near the mighty ocean.

Who am I with? My wife, Sheryl, is still as beautiful as the day I first met her on July 6, 1985. I'm grateful that we took our covenant seriously, until death do us part, for better or for worse, in sickness and in health. For the last fifty-three years, we have worked hard to create a marriage that endured tough times, major illness, and times of doubt. And now we celebrate our love often with our friends who journeyed the same path.

What have my children become? My sons, Jonathan and Matthew, are balanced, confident, successful professionals. They are generous, loving husbands, dads, and perhaps even granddads. Both are firm believers, and they are fervently committed to their faith in God. They have achieved manhood with strong character, healthy self-esteem, and a passion for their families and for adventure.

What am I doing? Sheryl and I are reclining in lounge chairs at the beach, hand in hand, discussing our boys and their families, our many blessings, and our next adventure. As we talk and laugh and our eyes fill with soft tears of contentment and joy, we are enjoying the magnificent beauty of God's hand-painted ocean sunset for what seems like the ten-thousandth time. And it has never grown old to us.

What do I want? To live out the rest of my days with an unwavering love for Sheryl and our three-generation family. To remain a man of integrity and commitment, no matter what happens. To help another person understand his or her value and God-given talents. To share my faith with whomever will listen.

How do I feel? Fulfilled and full of joy; but no less passionate about my life purpose than when I was thirty years old. I am hopeful that there might be one more life that God will allow me to impact. For the last fifty years, I have pursued with passion a career in teaching people how to be true sales professionals and how to balance their careers with an abundant life. Now I feel overwhelmingly privileged to have been God's instrument in helping people secure careers, save marriages, revitalize relationships, achieve success, maintain integrity, and pursue spiritual intimacy with Him. I am still eagerly awaiting more opportunities—even at my advanced age.

As you can see, this exercise really gets to the heart of the matter. It unearths why being a great sales trainer is important to me. (And it will reveal why being a great salesperson is important to you.) When I imagine my life as an eighty-year-old, I just can't see myself eagerly awaiting my next bank statement or counting a stack of one-hundred-dollar bills with my grandkids or gleefully reminiscing with my sons about the day I became a millionaire or billionaire or trillionaire. Is money important? Sure it is. We all need provision to live. Is more money a fair reward for working hard and smart? Of course it is. But it's not my core motive for speaking or writing or helping salespeople. And it won't be what brings me joy and fulfillment when I'm old.

Making a difference in your life and in the lives of my family will. Sharing my faith in God will. Helping you discover your purpose in life will. Showing you how to become a great salesperson *and* an even better person will. Teaching you how to add value to clients *and* to your spouse, son, and daughter will. These are the things that get me out of bed in the morning. These are the things that fire me up the night before a speaking event. These are my motives for becoming the best sales trainer and author I can possibly be. And you know what? The moment I forget these things and look to something more superficial to keep me motivated is the same moment I will begin to lose momentum *in* my career and enthusiasm *about* my career. And the same will be true of you . . . unless you're willing to get to the heart of the matter and stay there.

EXPLOITING EXTERNAL STIMULATION

Most salespeople struggle with motivation fluctuation. We all have days when we're sick or tired or just feel like playing hooky and going to the beach or the mall or the movies. And these feelings are not the result of hyping. Hyping happens to those who fail to link external stimulation with their internal motives for selling. Those salespeople have the most difficulty getting out of bed each day or picking up the phone one more time or visiting one more prospect. And for some, the lack of motivation can be a fatal blow to the sales job or, worse, to the sales career. But for those of you reading this book, that should no longer be an alternative.

Hyping goes away when real motives come into focus. And the key to keep hyping out of the picture is to become consistent and deliberate about selling from a foundation of your core motives. When your success in sales is measured by your ability to sell in a motive-centered manner, you won't have difficulty remaining enthusiastic—even when the sales seas rise and the sales winds begin to blow. And that's what you have to remember now, before we move on to the next mistake. If you're guilty of trying to hype your way through your sales career—even a little bit—it's time to stop and evaluate what you're really relying on to keep yourself motivated. Whatever it is, if it's superficial to your core motives, you're traveling down a dead-end street. And no salesperson wants to go there.

In the beloved American film *It's a Wonderful Life*, George Bailey (played by Jimmy Stewart) is on the verge of giving up on life.

(And maybe you feel that way about your sales career right now.) George believes that he is worth more to his family dead than he is alive, so he secretly prepares to commit suicide on Christmas Eve to avoid any more of life's difficulties and disappointments. But something happens. A heavenly visitor (Henry Travers) arrives and gives George the opportunity to peer at his life as an outsider—to see what life would be like if he had never been born. And George discovers something he didn't see before. He finds that his position in life affords him the opportunity to add value to many people's lives. He realizes that he is needed and genuinely appreciated, and that his relationships are very valuable commodities. He realizes that his life truly does make a difference.

As many of you who have seen the film know, George Bailey's new perspective reignites his passion to live, and he reenters life with a true, sustaining motivation to make the most out of living. Why? Because he finally grasps his core motive to live. And for many of you reading this book right now, that's precisely what you need in order to ignite your passion to continue selling. Like George Bailey, you need to step back and look at your (selling) life from a new perspective. You need to look closely and determine what makes you passionate about being a salesperson. Then you need to add your core motive(s) to your equation for success so that you no longer invest your hard-earned dollars and precious time on things that just add up to a lot of disappointing hype in the end. When you can do that, you'll be on the right path to a long-lasting, highly exhilarating career in sales. That's because all true sales success begins when you consistently tap into your core motives.

CHAPTER TWO

Mistake #2: Posing

Trying to sell before training to sell

T rick or treat? It's the question we hear every fall when Halloween rolls around. Adults attend costume parties, and children, with the key question on the tips of their tongues, hit the neighborhood streets in hopes of returning home with a sack full of goodies. Can you remember what costume you wanted to wear when you were young? When I was a kid, most boys wanted to dress up as a fireman, policeman, or ballplayer. Most girls back then wanted to be a princess, ballerina, or nurse. Off we went door to door, asking for sugary handouts. And we usually got what we wanted, didn't we? It's too bad the sales profession doesn't work that way.

Unfortunately many salespeople still think it does. Salespeople like Rick, a vacuum cleaner salesperson whose prospects weren't amused by his costume.

Rick had spent several minutes demonstrating the cutting-edge features of his vacuum and selling the prospects on his justification for a higher-priced, higher-quality product. Yet the prospects objected to the price. While Rick knew that he could sell the vacuum for a lower price, he thought a "special discount" from the head honcho would be a better way to offer it. So, instead of being forthcoming about the price, he decided to put on his best "in good with the boss" costume. Subsequently he asked his prospects if he could use their phone to discuss the price with his manager. And that's where his problems began.

Instead of dialing all seven numbers of his boss's phone number, Rick dialed only six. He knew his boss wouldn't appreciate the call. But he figured that a friendly (but phony) call with upper management would give him credibility with his prospects and maybe convince them that the lower price was a special favor from the boss. With his costume tightly buttoned up, Rick pretended he was talking, laughing, and negotiating with his boss on the other end of the phone. He was pretty convincing too. That is, until his costume fell off in a very untimely fashion. After a few minutes of ad-libbing his way through the call, the phone started making a loud beeping noise—you know, the one that phones make when they've been off the hook for too long. And the prospects heard it . . . loud and clear. In one very revealing instant, the prospects could see straight through Rick's disguise. And without hesitation, they asked him to leave . . . taking no treat with him.

Rick learned the hard way that when you get a sales job, you can't just put on a salesperson costume, go door to door, and expect prospects to slap some green goodies in your palm. Sure, just as you experienced in your younger days, your costume will probably evoke some heartfelt laughter, but I guarantee you it won't be because you're cute. More than likely the laughter will be followed by a door in your face or a dial tone on the other end of the phone. Enough of that kind of reaction and you'll eventually lose more than a good prospect; you'll end up losing your confidence and maybe even your job. It's a fate that many salespeople suffer. But it's the inevitable result of a fatal mistake I call "posing."

UNMASKING A MAJOR SELLING MISTAKE

Posing is any selling action that precedes selling education. It's trying to sell before actually training to sell. It's trying to act like a salesperson when you don't know what it takes to be a salesperson—whether or not the customer knows you're acting. And in the merciless world of sales, posing is the equivalent of putting on a clown suit and jumping into a corral with a two-thousand-pound rodeo bull. You may get by for a little while, but you'll eventually run out of barrels to hide behind—and you'll end up with a sharp horn in your backside.

> **In the merciless world of sales, posing is the equivalent of putting on a clown suit and jumping into a corral with a two-thousand-pound rodeo bull.**

The problem of posing begins for many salespeople when they are hired for their first sales job. Sales recruiters for large firms are notorious for hiring new blood with one thing in mind—production. The bottom line. The welcome message many salespeople are given is, "If you don't produce, you don't keep your job." And so they're given only a few days of training, if any, because heaven forbid that their employer not get an *immediate* return on the investment. And then off they go with their sales suits on, door to door or otherwise, not knowing much of anything about how to sell effectively. And what usually happens? About one-third don't make it more than a couple of months—and who can blame them? However, a slightly larger percentage do make it . . . with costumes, mirrors, and makeup. They figure out that if they tell prospects what they want to hear, they can keep their ear longer—whether or not what they are saying is true. They discover that if they create a façade that gives them credibility with a prospect, they can sometimes talk the individual into buying. They figure out that if they act as though they're selling the hottest product on the market, prospects want to know more—whether or not the people really need what they have to offer. And thus, sales costumes are created, and posing becomes second nature to many salespeople.

The film *Boiler Room,* which came out in 2000, provides an upsetting, coarse illustration of how posing can play out in the world of sales. It's the story of a nineteen-year-old named Seth (played by Giovanni Ribisi) who wants to move on and up in the world and somehow win the approval of his stiff, unforgiving father whom he adores. An opportunity comes knocking (literally) at his door when Seth meets Greg (Nicky Katt), a senior broker for J. T. Marlin, a Long Island stock brokerage. Seth is lured to work for the same hard-selling brokerage and soon finds himself amid a crowd of eager—and for the most part, naive—salesmen, who are promised fast cars, fine women, and loads of cash if they'll just play by the company's rules and sell stock like they've never sold before. "People come to this firm," they are told by the head trainer, "for one reason: to become filthy rich. That's it." And so Seth sees the firm as an opportunity to make up for his past mistakes and make a name for himself.

The following is an excerpt from the film in which Seth, as part of his training, is being instructed by the senior broker, Greg, on how to make successful cold calls when selling the firm's stock offerings. After listening in on one of Seth's failed cold-calling attempts and telling him how bad he is, Greg asserts the following:

> I have this friend who runs this other firm, right? He hands this book out to all his new trainees, right? It's called a rebuttal book.

It looks like a little File-O-Fax. It's got these index tabs, but instead of having letters like A–B or G–H, it has all these different things like—you know—"My wife won't let me" or "I'm not in the market right now" or "Send me a prospectus." It has a rebuttal for any excuse. Anyway, that's all stuff you're gonna have to learn later. The most important thing you gotta know right now is that you can be whomever you wanna be on the phone. You know what I'm saying. I mean, who cares? Do what you gotta do. Change your last name. Say you're the !@#$! vice president. You know. Who cares?

What Seth doesn't know in the beginning is that the small Long Island brokerage is really a scam. No one is telling the truth. The entire brokerage is a pose. None of the projected returns really exist. In fact, the products for which the stocks are being sold are unsubstantiated, made up, or failing, making the stock virtually worthless to the investors. The salespeople, we come to find out, are just being used as posers in a very large and lucrative game of sales trickery. And what's worse is that most of them don't mind—after all, they think they're gonna get rich. But if you've seen the film, you know that the results aren't nearly as pleasant as promised. In the end the brokerage is raided, money-hungry salespeople are arrested, and customers' lives are left in shambles by what seemed on the surface to simply be a shrewd selling strategy.

THE SIX SIGNS OF
IMPROVISATIONAL SELLING

As a result of perpetual posing, many salespeople like those in the film *Boiler Room* become really good at acting their way through selling efforts. Like movie stars who switch from one role to the next, many salespeople have become skilled at changing costumes and playing a wide range of characters to get into the pockets of their customers. But while a diverse character arsenal in the acting profession usually leads to more money, in the sales profession it usually leads to instability, increased stress, and ruined lives. When you've been a poser too long, the only way to put an end to it is to be forthright—something that will cause rickety sales relationships to tumble. But then again, remodeling one's career sometimes means knocking down a few unstable walls. And maybe that's what you need to do now.

Whether posing has become a standard or rare practice in your sales efforts, it nevertheless leads to a destructive, stressful sales career—and eventually to your demise. And I've found that posing is usually evident in a salesperson's career by the following six signs. As you read the list, ask yourself if any of the signs are characteristic of your selling endeavors. If you find that some are prevalent in your career, it's time to hang up your sales costumes and close the closet door behind you.

1. FALSE CONFIDENCE

Fake it till you make it is a dangerous way to close sales. Unfortunately, as we've already discussed, that's how many of us learned to sell. The result of not having proper sales training is that in the process of developing a wide array of characters to help you close sales, you never cultivate a genuine self-image. Your confidence in closing sales is erroneously based on your ability to fake a relationship rather than foster a relationship. And when the sales winds begin to whirl and all you have to rely on are the clients to whom you've sold before, you'll find that your confidence is nothing more than a house of cards. Our vacuum salesman learned this.

He was flying high for a few moments—but his confidence lasted only as long as his phony phone call.

To be successful in sales, you need the right kind of confidence—not the kind of swagger that comes from arrogance or pretense. You need confidence that your words to customers can be backed up by legitimate action. You need confidence that you can deliver *more* than is expected every time. When you start changing your story as often as your underpants, you'll eventually find that you have nothing but your closet of characters to count on in tough times. As a result, your sales career will always follow, like a caboose, the up-and-down train of the market.

> **To be successful in sales, you need the right kind of confidence—not the kind of swagger that comes from arrogance or pretense.**

2. ACCIDENTAL SUCCESS

At many of my speaking events I tell the audience that any success that is not based on an integrity-centered plan is accidental. In other words, if you can finagle your way to a sale, your success didn't happen as a natural course of action. It happened by a lucky guess and a roll of the dice. It happened by chance. And relying on chance sales leads only to erratic success. We'll discuss this in further detail in the upcoming chapters, but for now understand that the more you rely on accidental sales success, the longer and harder you have to work to be successful—and the less likely you are to be satisfied. Like one client of mine named Glenn who still puts in about eighty hours a week, despite being advised otherwise.[1] He makes good money, yes. But it's no accident that he's not happy, and his personal life since becoming a salesperson is a study in loss, shame, and irresponsibility. He's become such a poser that even his off-the-job relationships are fake. There's not much genuine in his life anymore because his dependence on posing has gotten way out of hand.

The truth is that when selling is based on integrity, success can be predicted with a fairly high degree of certainty. If you ever studied the topic of probability in school, you know that as the number of factors in a given set of circumstances increases, the probability of a specific outcome decreases. For example, if you have one golden egg and one white egg in a bag, there is a 50 percent probability that you will pull the golden egg from the bag, or 50-50 odds. Very good odds. But if you have a bag full of twenty different-colored eggs and only one of them is gold, the probability of pulling out the golden egg decreases dramatically to only 5 percent, or 20-1 odds. And that's what happens with posing. The more consistently you bring the same "golden egg" set of factors to a selling effort (integrity, professionalism, and reliability), the more probable a golden-egg outcome remains. On the other hand, with every new pose and posture you add to your bag of selling tricks, a golden-egg outcome becomes less and less probable, or more and more haphazard.

The only way to gain stability in your sales career is to learn the most productive way to sell and then repeat that effort every time. Posing will never meet this criterion because it is neither productive nor consistent. And if you're thinking that you can just wear one sales costume that works again and again, you're wrong. Not every audience will buy into the same act. Thinking the same sales costume will win everyone over is like thinking a gorilla suit will win over both an audience of five-year-olds and an audience of real gorillas. If you don't change your costume to suit your audience, you'll probably get eaten alive. And who wants to deal with that risk?

The bottom line is that unwavering sales success is maintained by consistency. Consistent actions on your part lead to consistent expectations on the customer's part . . . which lead to consistent reactions from the customer . . . which lead to consistent results in the sales transaction. Arbitrary actions will lead only to arbitrary reactions and results. And you can't build a stable sales career arbitrarily.

3. Selling Reluctance

Salespeople who suffer from call reluctance fall into one of two categories: (1) those who don't believe in what they are selling, or (2) those who don't believe in their ability to sell. And let me add something here: believing in your ability to "white lie" your way through a sale does not count. Rick, the vacuum salesperson, believed in his little routine—and it got him nothing but a shove out the door. There is a way to sell successfully with integrity and sincerity, and if you don't know how to do that, you are most certainly relying on a phony form of salesmanship that will always lead to reluctance.

If it's your product that you don't believe in, then you're in the same boat. Selling something that is either second-rate or not needed by your prospects does not breed confidence before making a call. And it shouldn't. It's like trying to get excited about selling a bike to a fish. That's nothing to find assurance in.

On the other hand, if you've been duped by your employer into selling a substandard product or service, then you need to get out of that position. I rarely recommend that salespeople quit their jobs because it's usually more difficult to rebuild than remodel, but sometimes it's necessary. A friend of mine was once recruited to sell household-cleaning and personal-hygiene products. But when he wasn't impressed with the quality of the stuff, he got out, and he didn't look back. Make a point to always sell something that you can really be proud of selling—something that you are certain can really add value to people's lives. With that commitment, combined with some solid sales training and practice, you'll quickly do away with selling reluctance.

4. Underperforming Clients

Probably the most obvious indication of posing is the lack of performance by a salesperson's clientele. When you give your clients no reason (or a phony reason) to trust you, you also give them no reason to return to you or refer you to others. Think about an experience with a salesperson whose motives you didn't quite trust. Let's assume you bought from that salesperson reluctantly and only because you had already spent so much time at that place of business. Would you be excited to give that person more business when a need for that product arose again? I doubt it. Would you even think about sending your family and friends to that person? Again, I doubt it.

The problem with posing is that if it leads to sales, most often it leads to one-time sales. Therefore, as a poser, you're always stuck in an acquisition mode instead of a retention mode where sales success gains momentum. And if you can't gain momentum with existing clients, your success will always be short-lived.

5. Overworking

Working eighty hours a week is not a prerequisite to being a successful sales professional. Unfortunately posing leads to a tendency toward working harder and longer than necessary in order to close sales. Multiplied over time, that leads to more hours on the job to meet your goals. Posing is a hit-and-miss approach to selling. If one costume doesn't work on the prospect, then you have to try on another. If the second one doesn't work, then you have to try on the third. And all that does in the end is to decrease your overall productivity and increase your hours on the job. Eventually, because you're posing so often on the job, like Glenn, you have trouble being genuine off the job.

> **Working eighty hours a week is not a prerequisite to being a successful sales professional.**

Over the years many sales books have preached that you must always be closing in order to get lots of sales. And that notion leads to an inclination to try this method and that method until something sticks. Not only is that advice a bunch of hogwash, but it's unproductive and extremely damaging to your career. Such advice often translates into the impulse that if being forthright doesn't work, then maybe a little fib will close the deal; and if a little fib won't close the deal, then maybe an all-out lie will. Eventually you're stuck in a cycle of both inefficiency and duplicity. And that cycle will ultimately spin out of your control.

6. JOB TURNOVER

For most salespeople, posing leads to short-lived sales positions. The only problem is that many sales professionals point an accusing finger at other things when jobs don't work out instead of pointing at a mirror. Posers mistakenly believe that joining a new company, selling a new product, or moving to a new territory will improve their sales results. They don't realize that they're placing all the colored eggs (from point #2) back into the bag and hoping their probability for drawing out the one golden egg will change. Of course, it won't. Their probability for success remains low as long as they continue to bring haphazard factors to their selling efforts. All they are doing by starting over with a new position, product, or territory is reshuffling the same colored eggs and hoping for different results. It just won't work.

THE ONUS OF SELLING SUCCESS

By making the mistake of trying to pose your way to the top, you are ultimately putting the onus of selling success on your ability to role-play—to play the part of an interested, caring, genuine salesperson. And let's be honest: when salespeople are interested only in closing the sale, they are not good actors—whether they admit it or not. If you saw the film *Analyze That*, you probably remember an amusing depiction of what can happen when a presumptuous salesperson tries to act the part of a trustworthy salesperson. As the film illustrates, what often ends up happening is that the salesperson's true colors begin to show.

The quick-tempered, irreverent mob boss Paul Vitti (Robert De Niro) has feigned insanity in prison to get released early into the care of his reluctant psychotherapist, Dr. Ben Sobel (Billy Crystal). As part of his patient's treatment, Dr. Sobel refers Vitti to a friend's placement agency where the mafioso is given an "honest" job selling luxury cars.

We pick up the movie as the unsympathetic Vitti is finishing up what we come to learn has been a tedious, hour-long sales pitch to a middle-aged, well-to-do couple. And both his patience and his pose are beginning to wear thin.

Vitti:	Look at the size of that trunk. You could put three bodies in there . . . just kidding. Just trying to levitate the situation.
Man:	[*Starting to walk away*] Okay—thank you. We appreciate it.
Vitti:	[*Interrupting*] Sure, sure. Hey, what kinda car you's drive anyway?
Man:	[*Stopping and turning back to Vitti*] Uh, it's a Lexus 430 LS.
Vitti:	[*Sarcastically*] That's like a—Toyota?
Man:	[*Unamused*] It's—a Lexus.
Vitti:	[*Irreverently*] Yeah, Toyota, Lexus . . . same thing. Japanese, right? Let's not forget Pearl Harbor. Anyway, let's get serious. You wanna buy this car or what? Yea or nay?
Woman:	[*Matter-of-factly*] Well, I don't know. We have to think about it.
Vitti:	[*Beginning to grow impatient*] What's there to think about? I mean, you told me you liked it. You asked me *ten thousand* questions. I answered *every* single one of them. You drove it. You love it. What more do you need to know?
Man:	[*Taking his wife's hand and turning to walk away again*] You know—that's a lot of money. And, uh, we just need the time to consider it.
Vitti:	[*Frustrated*] Consider it? Well, why don't you consider this? You've been [wearing me down] for about an hour, asking me about every !@#$! accessory in this car: *What about the light? . . . What about this? . . . What about that?*

Woman:	[*Interrupting*] Look, you *cannot* talk to customers like that.
Vitti:	[*Arrogantly*] You're not customers as far as I'm concerned. You wanna buy the car or not?
Man:	[*Pointing to Vitti*] Not from *you*! I want to see the manager.

Clearly, although posing as a lunatic got him released from prison, Paul Vitti was not nearly as good at posing his way to success as a salesperson. And neither will you. Despite the number of roles you think you can play, your success as a salesperson will never reach its potential if you don't learn to do away with a reliance on posing in your career. Posing is not productive closing.

The most obvious reason that the mistake is toxic to your selling career is that role-playing in sales is usually rooted in outright deception or just plain pretext—hiding your true agenda. The less obvious but equally toxic reason that posing fails to sustain success is that it cannot meet the criteria for maintaining long-term relationships with clients. Trust must be at the core of any and every client relationship in order for you to realize the full, lifetime value of every client. Posing prohibits you from building trustworthy relationships and, therefore, sustaining your clients' trust for the long haul.

While trying to pose your way to sales success, you may become really good at role-playing, really good at telling half-truths, really good at convincing people that you're something you're not. But in the process of becoming a good poser, you never hone the tools of selling that are necessary to reap a true harvest every year. Posing teaches you to change like a chameleon in every selling situation in order to close the sale; posing doesn't teach you what to do in order to keep the client. Posing can give you only one part of the equation for success: getting a sale. Posing fails as a selling practice when it comes to following up and fostering relationships after a sale.

For example, it's easy to give a prospect the impression that you are an avid golfer because it gives you credibility to land the sale. It's a lot more complicated when that person becomes your regular client and asks you to golf every other week, especially when you've only been golfing once in your life. When you lose twelve balls on the first three holes, your client will know you didn't just forget to bring your "A" game. And that's precisely what happens when you pose your way to a sale. Can you imagine what would happen if you inserted multiple clients into that scenario? Then the juggling becomes nearly impossible. That's why Algernon Sidney once quipped that "liars ought to have good memories."

Posing is the notion that sales success is just a matter of feeding the right lines to prospects—it's similar to the notion that a cheesy guy uses when he tries to one-line his way to a date with a pretty girl. And the problem with that notion is that if you do finagle your way to a sale (or a date), the role-playing doesn't end. In order to maintain the relationship, you must continue to pose. And if your lines weren't wholly based on truth, you're in for a hard time. Knowing a bunch of one-liners won't cut it. That's because a bunch of witty lines won't build authentic trust, and trust is the foundation of every successful sales relationship. Something Linda Rudd understands very well.

Before Linda made the transition to her current sales position in the mortgage industry, she had spent several years in an industry where posing is a fast track to failure. She worked as a private banking and trust portfolio manager, which basically meant that if clients

were going to pay for her services, trust was not only recommended—
it was essential. Her clients needed to trust her with their very liveli-
hoods, with everything they were worth. And they did. The majority
of her clients (90 percent) had a net worth in excess of $1 million.
All told, she managed a total of $125 million of her clients' assets.
Clearly she was doing more than posing her way to scattered success. Her clients trusted her implicitly, and to show it, they placed
their futures in her hands. As a result of her trust-building training
and experience, succeeding in her second career as a mortgage originator was not only a snap; it was a huge success.

Once Linda learned the ropes of the real estate industry, she
went about her job just as she had learned to do in her previous
position: she began building trust with customers. "From my first
job," she says, "I already understood that if I was going to land
key accounts with the best customers, I needed to show them I
could be counted on." And that's what she did. While most customers calling on mortgage originators are primarily interested in
learning the going interest rate—especially in a market like
today's—Linda understood that she needed to do more than clev-
erly recite rates to customers in order to establish trust-based relationships with them.

Instead of just putting on her best smiling voice and answering
a bunch of her customers' queries, Linda turned the tables around.
"Let me learn a little bit about you and where you are right now"
became a common phrase in her introductory talks with customers.
She then went on to explain to her customers that she was willing
and ready to serve them in whatever capacity they desired, but she
could not do that without understanding their motives for seeking a
mortgage. That was the only way, she stated, that she could meet
their needs and expectations for many years to come. And customers

began responding in a positive fashion. They shared their motives, values, and needs where a mortgage was concerned, and in doing so, they entrusted Linda with the keys to their business. And Linda has opened many doors along the way.

Since becoming a mortgage sales professional, Linda's gross sales have exploded by an average of 64 percent per year. Take a look at her progression of success:

Year 1	$13 million in sales
Year 2	$26 million in sales
Year 3	$42 million in sales
Year 4	$55 million in sales

Now in her fifth year as a mortgage originator, Linda is projected to close more than $75 million in sales—nearly six times her first-year total. If you think that posing your way to sales success is the quickest and most profitable path . . . think again.

To avoid posing in your sales career and progress toward your true success potential, you need to approach selling as Linda does. First, you need to do away with the notion that you can build a successful and lasting sales career on anything short of integrity. You simply cannot. Second, you must make an ongoing effort to communicate in the true language of selling. Something Linda does well.

Do away with the notion that you can build a successful and lasting sales career on anything short of integrity. You simply cannot.

LEARNING THE RIGHT LANGUAGE, NOT THE RIGHT LINES

When it comes to training for true sales success, it's really a matter of learning the language of selling as opposed to learning clever selling lines. Two things come to mind when considering the defining characteristics of a language. First, language is usually the most common characteristic of a specific group of people. (For example, the most common characteristic of Americans is that we speak English. The most common characteristic of Mexicans is that they speak Spanish.) Second, a common language is necessary for two or more people to communicate in the most effective manner. You know this firsthand if you've ever visited a foreign country in which you didn't know the language. You probably made a lot of hand motions and exaggerated facial expressions to get your point across. And I think you'd agree that is not exactly the most productive approach. But that's just what happens when you try to communicate in a language that is foreign to the native language of selling.

To do away with posing and close sales in an effective manner, you must communicate in the language that is most easily understood by your prospects and clients, and that language is trust. There is no better path to a sale than to communicate trustworthiness to your prospects and clients. More than any characteristic, trust is the definitive common ground in the world of sales. If you communicate trust, your prospects more easily understand you, your clients more readily receive you, and you more fluently maintain your existing relationships. No hand motions, exaggerated facial expressions, or costumes are needed to get your point across. And when you clearly communicate trust, trust is clearly communicated back to you in the form of positive responses, repeat sales, and solid referrals. Communicating to a prospect in a language contrary to trust is like trying to convince a fish to take your bait. No matter what you say, you won't get many bites.

To communicate trust to your prospects, you can rely on five traits that can be explained with the acronym T.R.U.S.T. If you convey these five traits consistently, your prospects will be much more receptive to what you say.

1. TIMELINESS.

So much of what the common salesperson communicates has to do with schedules and whims. As a result, prospects have to listen to long rants about product details that may or may not be important to them. They receive calls they are not expecting. They don't get call backs when the calls were promised. And what it all conveys is that the salesperson's time is more important than the prospects' time. If you want to convey trust, don't ever assume prospects have time to talk to you. Schedule only what you intend to maintain. Call only when your prospect expects it. And don't ever assume prospects want to hear you say anything without first asking.

2. RELEVANCE.

"What does that have to do with my needs?" is a far-too-common question in the world of sales. And whether prospects verbalize it or not, many still think it. To communicate trust to your prospects, don't ever go into a selling situation assuming you know what they need. Let them tell you what is relevant. Make listening your first priority when you deal with prospects. Then, with their permission, share proposed solutions based on what they've told you, not what you think they want.

3. UNDERSTANDING.

If you pose your way to a sale, your focus is on the performance. But when posing is not an option, you are forced to ascertain needs in order to provide a compelling presentation. If prospects don't think you are trying to understand their situation before you try to sell something to them, you might as well forget their business.

4. SINCERITY.

I'm only going to say this once in this book because I shouldn't need to say it anymore: if you can't be yourself in selling situations, then you shouldn't be a salesperson. Nobody likes a phony. Nobody likes a poser. If you can't stand it when a presumptuous salesperson invades your space, why would you ever think that others would enjoy it? (Now if you're just a presumptuous person, that's an entirely separate problem that can't be fixed within the world of selling.) But to be successful in the sales profession, you must get past your pretense and treat your customers with respect.

5. THOROUGHNESS.

Integrity and professionalism really show up here. To convey trust, be thorough in everything you do. Always cover all your prospects' bases for them. Never make them wait for you to "get back to them." Never make them ask you for a progress update. As much as possible, have everything they need to do in order to give you business—and more business—lined up and ready to go. That's not presumption; that's professionalism. From your explanation of the contract to a simple phone call to apprise them of an order's progress, nothing will make your prospects and clients more certain of your ability to meet their needs (and those of their friends and colleagues) than being thorough.

REMAINING FLUENT

There's one more thing to be said before we move on. If you've ever learned a new language, you know one thing to be true: if you don't speak the language regularly, you lose it. You don't remain fluent in any language unless you continue to use it in everyday conversation. And the same is true of the language of trust.

To eliminate posing *immediately,* you must learn to communicate *clearly* in the language of trust. In other words, the five traits listed here must be evident by the way you sell. Then to eliminate posing *permanently,* you must learn to communicate *regularly* in the language of trust. After all, if you're truly interested in lasting sales success, you can't foster trust with one client and not another. Building lifetime relationships with every client must be your goal. And the only way to do that is to communicate trust consistently to every one of your clients on a regular basis. Speak the language clearly and regularly so that it remains second nature.

And you know what will happen if you succeed in doing that? You'll find that the more you communicate in the language of trust, the easier your sales will come and the longer your relationships will last. No longer will you have to rely on a wide array of poses to convince your prospects to buy from you. In fact, you will eventually come to a place where all you have to do to remain highly successful is to foster trustworthy relationships with your existing clients, like my good friend and client Tim Broadhurst whom I mentioned in my last book. He spends all of his selling time fostering the trust-centered relationships he's built with a mere twelve clients. No smoke and mirrors got him to that place. He built each of those twelve relationships with honesty, professionalism, and mutual respect. And those twelve relationships now bring his company nearly $100 million in sales every year. Furthermore, they allow Tim and his family fifteen weeks of vacation a year. You think he's glad he didn't rely on posing to succeed in sales? You bet.

Communicating consistently in the language of trust will not only eliminate posing from your selling routine—and that's a must if you're serious about making sales your lifetime career—it will also usher in a selling prosperity you've never had before. As the adage says, honesty really is the best policy.

CHAPTER THREE

Mistake #3: Tinkering

*Treating the symptoms but not the sickness
of poor selling efforts*

Recently I took a trip to the local drugstore because I was curious about something. Of all the medicinal products on the shelves, how many do you suppose treat actual sicknesses, and how many do you suppose treat the symptoms of sicknesses? I'll tell you. Of the 511 different medicinal products on the "Cold and Cough" aisle at the local Longs drugstore here in my hometown, 485 products treat symptoms and only 26 treat the actual root of the sickness. Go to your local drugstore and I'm sure you'll come up with about the same percentage. That's 95 percent! Have we become a nation of symptomatic maniacs?

Certainly there is a time and place to treat symptoms, namely, when we're in the process of treating the sickness. When we've hurt ourselves and are on the way to getting our wounds treated, we take something to ease the pain or do something to stop the bleeding. Of course, there is value in treating symptoms. But if we're honest, more often than not we rely too heavily on symptomatic treatments, and we overlook the sickness.

The truth is that many of us love temporary fixes. We order them from commercials, catalogs, and magazines because we think they are the answer to our problems. We buy 'em up because when we're feeling bad, we just want to *feel* better—we don't think much about actually *being* better. That takes too long. And heaven forbid we actually do something proactive to prevent sickness from happening in the first place. For most busy people, fixing the real problem is too much to ask. "Just gimme something to get me through" has become the motto of many.

Unfortunately it seems that motto has spilled over into the sales profession. "Just gimme something to get me through" sounds a lot like the approach of many sales professionals to their selling problems. Sometimes entire companies take this symptomatic approach to solving problems. That's certainly how the German-based drug maker, Bayer Corporation, tried to deal with a very big dilemma—and it cost the firm big time. In fact, it's still costing them.

In the mid-1980s, Bayer subsidiary Cutter Biological introduced a blood-clotting medicine for hemophiliacs. The medicine, known as Factor VIII concentrate, provided the ingredient that hemophiliacs' blood needs in order to clot. By injecting themselves with Factor VIII, hemophiliacs could essentially stop bleeding completely, allowing them to carry on normal lives. It was praised as a wonder drug for those suffering from hemophilia. And when the drug was initially marketed, it was well received. However, there was one major problem. To produce the medicine, Bayer had used pools of plasma from more than ten thousand donors, and since the plasma donations were given prior to sophisticated screening for the AIDS virus, they had a high risk of containing HIV. It was a serious problem that needed to be addressed. But instead of fixing the problem immediately by taking the drug off the market, Bayer continued to make and sell Factor VIII while simultaneously creating and selling a safer drug. The company tried to brush the real problem under the rug for the sake of profits.

According to a *New York Times* investigation in 2003, "By continuing to sell the old version of the life-saving medicine, documents show [the company] was trying to avoid being stuck with large stocks of a product that was increasingly unmarketable in the U.S. and Europe."[1] It seems that addressing its potential investment risk was more important to Bayer than addressing the potential loss of lives. Fixing profits seemed more important than fixing people. In fact, the *Times* report revealed that all told, Bayer "appears to have exported more than 100,000 vials of unheated concentrate, worth more than $4 million, after it began selling the safer product." And because Bayer skirted its real selling problem—a potentially unsafe product—its problem became much bigger.

To date, Bayer and the three other companies that made the concentrate have paid hemophiliacs about $600 million to settle more than fifteen years of lawsuits. And the lawsuits aren't finished. On June 2, 2003, several hemophiliacs filed another giant lawsuit in San Francisco. And history suggests that the plaintiffs have a pretty good case. But the loss of money wasn't the worst of Bayer's consequences. According to the *Times* investigation, "AIDS was passed on to thousands of hemophiliacs, many of whom died, in one of the worst drug-related medical disasters in history." I wonder if Bayer still thinks it handled its problem correctly?

SOLVING ANYTHING BUT THE PROBLEM

What the Bayer Corporation did is something many salespeople do when it comes to problem solving. It's something I call "tinkering," and as in the case of Bayer, it will lead to disaster in your sales career if you don't change your ways.

Tinkering is trying to skirt your problems for the sake of more sales, then hoping you don't suffer the consequences. It's treating the symptoms of poor selling efforts instead of getting to the bottom of why they occurred in the first place and making sure they never happen again. It's like adding oil to your car engine every two weeks instead of repairing the crack in the oil pan. And when tinkering becomes a mainstay of your sales career, you eventually end up with more problems than you can fix in a single selling situation. As a result, you start losing more sales than you close. You start losing more clients. You start losing confidence. And if tinkering remains your problem-solving tendency long enough, you will start losing jobs.

As simple as it may sound, tinkering is probably the most common mistake salespeople make. I think you'd agree that many salespeople feel crunched for time. They have so many things they want and need to accomplish in a day that taking a break to evaluate and fix their selling practices seems out of the question. This mind-set is especially true during the last week of every month when quotas need to be met and expectations are at their highest. And so it goes that many salespeople just push through the problems that arise without ever really giving much thought to why they occurred or how they can be avoided the next time around. Eventually that strategy becomes habit. *Sell hard and fast, and if problems arise, just do what needs to be done to sustain momentum. Cover them up. Put a bandage on them, take some pain medication, and move on. No time to stop and assess the damage. Gotta close more sales. Gotta make more money . . .*

Although that might seem to work in the wide world of sports, it won't work in the wide world of sales.

The trouble with that problem-solving mentality is that when your selling practices are amiss, you're sustaining momentum in the wrong direction—even when you think you're moving forward. Then you are forced to work harder to achieve success. Think of it this way: when tinkering has become a habit, achieving success is like having to go around the entire block to get next door. It just adds a lot of unnecessary work and stress.

PUTTING TINKERING TO THE TEST

Jason and Andrew sell term life insurance for a nationally recognized company. Both are in their second year of selling, and both are very ambitious to do well. Both believe that their product is valuable, and both are excited when an individual purchases a policy. But there is a stark difference in their selling strategies and subsequently their selling futures.

Jason hates doing things the wrong way. He's passionate about discovering the best way to accomplish a task, then sticking with it. He spent much of his first year of selling evaluating everything he did, right or wrong. If something was working, he regularly asked, "Is this way the best way?" If something wasn't working, he immediately asked, "Why didn't this work?" and "How can I improve next time around?"

As a result of his commitment to constantly evaluate his sales processes and strategies, Jason's first year ended just a little above average. But he was on the upswing. With a solid strategy in place, he knew that he would improve in his second year. In fact, he had proof of it. Over the last three months of his first year, he had sold more policies than in his first nine months combined. His commitment was beginning to pay off. And he had three consecutive "Salesperson of the Month" awards to show for it.

Andrew, on the other hand, went about selling differently. He literally hit the ground running and didn't look back. He wanted to produce immediately—and produce he did . . . at least at first. In his first month of selling, he worked an average of sixty hours a week and was runner-up for "Salesperson of the Month" with the number of policies he sold. With the momentum from the first month of success, Andrew made it his goal to win the award in his second month.

But something happened that he hadn't counted on. What had worked the first month of selling wasn't working as well the second month. In fact, he was having to work harder to close sales—especially since he was no longer working off a prequalified list of prospects. But instead of putting his head in the sand and quitting, Andrew vowed to overcome what wasn't working by working harder and harder. *Everyone comes to roadblocks*, he told himself. *I just have to run through them.*

His sixty hours a week became seventy hours a week. It was the price he felt he had to pay in order to be highly successful. He was determined to succeed—no matter what it took. And when the end of the second month rolled around, Andrew had done fairly well. He hadn't won any awards, but he did manage to finish fourth in the running. His bosses were still impressed. And Andrew still felt he was on the right track. He vowed to put his nose back to the grindstone and make things work. Success, he hoped, would eventually come more easily.

But a funny thing happened. As the days became longer and the hours piled up, Andrew started becoming sloppy. His fatigue started to show. He began to forget names and account details and appointments—all things he tried to overcome by slapping on a clever Band-Aid and forging full steam ahead. But he couldn't deny that cracks had begun to show and sales had begun to slip through.

Andrew's status in the company slid until it steadied right around the middle of the salesperson pack. Some months he managed a few more sales than the others, but for the most part it seemed that his success scale had stabilized—and rust was starting to form. In his climb to the top of the sales ranks, Andrew had come to a lid on his success, and he wasn't sure how to lift it.

A TINKERING TELL-ALL

Have you ever felt the way Andrew did? After weeks, months, or even years of striving, you just can't seem to break through to major sales success. Do you feel that there's a lid on your success that you can't lift? If you have felt these things recently, it's very likely that you're suffering from the side effects of tinkering. And you may be surprised at how easily the little cracks in your sales efforts can creep in.

Review these common sales Band-Aids, and ask yourself if you've ever slapped one of them on and tried to forge ahead:

- Problem: Sales falling through
  Band-Aid: *Try to recover clients after sale has fallen through.*

- Problem: Objections
  Band-Aid: *Develop more scripts to overcome them.*

- Problem: Low sales
  Band-Aid: *Make more calls.*

- Problem: A lot to do and not a lot of time to do it
  Band-Aid: *Work harder.*

- Problem: Few to no referrals from existing clients
  Band-Aid: *Ask for referrals more often.*

- Problem: Poor prospect quality
  Band-Aid: *Make more calls.*

Sales Band-Aids are more common than most salespeople think, and many salespeople use them without ever knowing it. That's why tinkering is the most common mistake of sales professionals. Whether you're tinkering a little or a lot in your sales career, the bottom line is that your sales efforts are not as efficient and effective as they could be. To do away with tinkering once and for all, you have to first adjust your thinking. You have to do away with the notion that you can always quick-fix every problem that arises over the course of a specific selling effort. You can't. You have to get rid of the belief that working harder and longer can make up for your sales shortcomings. It won't. You have to stop thinking that more calls mean more business. They don't. Unless, of course, you want to continue to make more calls, deal with more unhappy clients, work more hours, and suffer more stress . . . and still fall short of your selling potential. I don't think anyone wants that.

Take another look at the sales Band-Aids that we discussed, this time with the proper prescription inserted at the end:

- Problem: Sales falling through
  Band-Aid: Try to recover clients after sale has fallen through.
  Prescription: *Survey clients before asking for business.*

- Problem: Objections
  Band-Aid: Develop more scripts to overcome them.
  Prescription: *Ascertain prospects' values and needs up front and prevent the objection.*

- Problem: Low sales
  Band-Aid: Make more calls.
  Prescription: *Improve call conversion by heeding the values and meeting the needs of prospects.*

- Problem: A lot to do and not a lot of time to do it
  Band-Aid: Work harder.
  Prescription: *Work smarter; become more productive.*

- Problem: Few to no referrals from existing clients
  Band-Aid: Ask for referrals more often.
  Prescription: *Provide better service and consistent follow-up.*

- Problem: Poor prospect quality
  Band-Aid: Make more calls.
  Prescription: *Prequalify prospects before pursuing them so that wasted calls are not made.*

When you look at things that way, it's easier to see the detrimental effects of tinkering, isn't it? And that's good because doing away with tinkering starts when you acknowledge your tendency toward it.

A NEW PHILOSOPHY OF HEALING

If you've ever stayed up late at night, you've probably noticed that the infomercials increase the later it gets. Have you ever wondered why that is? My off-the-cuff opinion has always been that the people at whom the infomercials are aimed usually can't sleep. Maybe that's not the case, but certainly those to whom they appeal are looking for answers to their problems. They don't know what they're missing; they just know they're missing something. They're so sick and tired of being sick and tired that they are desperately searching for something, anything, to make them better. Then they see an infomercial that promises them great wealth or better health or more happiness if they'll just make a simple phone call and invest a few dollars. And so many do, in hopes that they will finally fix what ails them.

But you know what? Most of the products that infomercials sell do nothing but put a short-term fix on a long-term problem. Most just cover the wound for a little while so you don't have to think about its being there. When the Band-Aid gets old and falls off, the wound is usually still there—maybe in the form of a scar. You're still broke or in bad shape or dissatisfied with your life. And if that's the way you've been trying to treat your sales problems—tinkering around the real issues—similar results have probably become common. If you've made the mistake long enough, you probably have a host of problems that you aren't even aware of. At one time in my career, that was certainly the case for me. I was a symptomatic maniac.

When I was in my twenties, I remember coming to the frustrating realization that the only thing I was doing consistently in my sales career was jumping from one problem to the next. I was constantly under maintenance. If it wasn't one thing, it was another. I was trying everything, anything, to improve my business. I was adding accounts and prospects, regardless of whether they were right for me or my business was right for them. I was spending more time in the field. I was trying to manage my time better. In one calendar year, I purchased *three* different time management systems in an attempt to gain control. But not *one* of them worked. I was focused on any treatment I could get my hands on—but it was rare that one led to a breakthrough. I thought the next hot seminar would do the trick, and I went to many, hoping for a miraculous healing. But when it came down to it, nothing did the trick. I didn't understand it then, but like many salespeople today, I had mastered the dangerous art of tinkering.

I'll be candid with you: nearly every salesperson has made the mistake of tinkering at one time or another in his or her career. The fact is that when most of us began selling, it was more important to produce sales than it was to perfect selling techniques. Most of us were more like Andrew than Jason. Like I used to be. When sales started to wane, we just got tough. We didn't stop to think much. We pushed our way through the problems so we could meet our quotas and goals. We moved forward two steps, but the truth was, we moved back two or three steps at the same time. And that's certainly not the most efficient or most productive method of advancing one's selling career.

When I finally came to terms with my faulty philosophy of problem solving and began disciplining myself to get to the root of my sales problems, things turned around dramatically in my career.

- I became one of the top salespeople in my firm.

- I reduced my client load by more than 50 percent while expanding revenues by more than 400 percent.

- I increased the amount of money I made per hour from hundreds to thousands.

- I received more referrals than I ever imagined.

- I began taking more than three months of vacation per year.

And if you're willing to adopt a new philosophy of sales problem solving as I did, believe you can do the same.

It's time to put away all the quick-fix, get-rich, bring-you-ultimate-happiness products and presuppositions, and commit to getting down to the real root of your sales problems. And I think you'll find that when you're willing to do that, increasing your sales success and satisfaction isn't far behind.

A NEW PROBLEM-SOLVING PRESCRIPTION

The first thing that's required to put an end to tinkering in your sales career is more philosophical than practical, but it is nonetheless a necessity. Furthermore, it's the first thing I did to begin advancing my sales career in the right direction. You have to make up your mind once and for all that it is more important that you *be* a better salesperson rather than just *feel* like a better salesperson. As you can see, there are major differences between the two:

FEELING BETTER	BEING BETTER
False confidence	Genuine confidence
Problem hidden	Problem solved
Increased work	Decreased work
Short-term success	Long-term stability

In other words, to put an end to tinkering and initiate a new approach to problem solving, you must believe for yourself that covering up the symptom of a sales problem is neither the best nor the quickest path to sales success, and that fixing the root of the problem is. When that philosophy becomes your own—when you remove tinkering as a spoke in the wheel of your success strategy—then you can begin to approach ongoing sales improvement the right way. And that's where mere problem solving becomes a means to increased sales productivity.

For top salespeople, increasing sales productivity begins with a clear understanding of how a successful sale should be constructed—from the ground up. They have an instruction manual firmly implanted in their minds that reminds them precisely what a successful sale looks like as each part is added to the picture. And the same must be true of you if you are to permanently overcome the temptation to tinker when something goes awry. It's one thing to commit to getting to the bottom of your problems when they arise. It's another thing to know when, where, and why a problem occurred. That begins when you understand the ingredients that make up a successful sale—from beginning to end.

If you don't know how something is correctly put together, then you will always have a difficult time knowing how to fix it. You will always be "guesstimating" your repairs. But in sales, you can't wing problem solving. As committed as you may be to getting to the root of the problem, you can't perform do-it-yourself repairs without the correct sales manual. It's like trying to perform brain surgery without knowing the anatomy of the brain. And in both instances, one mistake could be fatal.

For many mistaken salespeople, the construction of a sale commences when they pick up the phone to make a cold call or walk into an office without an appointment, and the construction of a sale is completed when the prospect gives a final yes or no. Their mental sales manual looks something like this:

INCORRECT SALES MANUAL

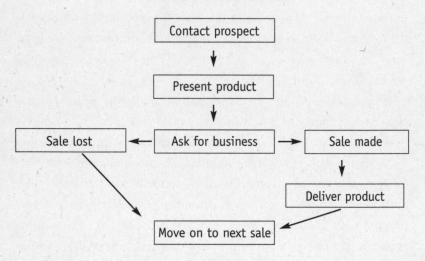

Not only is that a grossly insufficient sales strategy, but it also leaves you exposed and vulnerable to many potential problems, such as:

- Prolonged phone calls

- Uninterested prospects

- High-maintenance, low-profit prospects

- Constant objections

- Low conversion rate

- Lack of trust

- Lack of referrals

- Lack of repeat business

- Continual mode of acquisition

- More calls and longer hours to achieve success

Furthermore, an insufficient sales manual will leave you clueless when you try to ascertain the nature of a problem. It's a two-edged sword in that sense. With an improper mental sales manual, you will leave yourself wide open to problems because you are selling ineffectively, and you will make it virtually impossible to pinpoint and treat your problems in an efficient manner.

On the other hand, those who are met with perpetual success understand how a sale is constructed from beginning to end. For such achievers, a sale begins well before any words are spoken to a prospect, and the construction is never complete. In other words, the most successful salespeople strengthen the foundation of a sale before they ever attempt to sell—and by doing so they error-proof their selling process as much as possible *before* it starts. Eventually, like a top-dollar mechanic with his own vintage Mustang, successful salespeople are able to safeguard their sales from major problems with the preventative maintenance that quality craftsmanship provides. The sales manual in their minds looks like this:

CORRECT SALES MANUAL

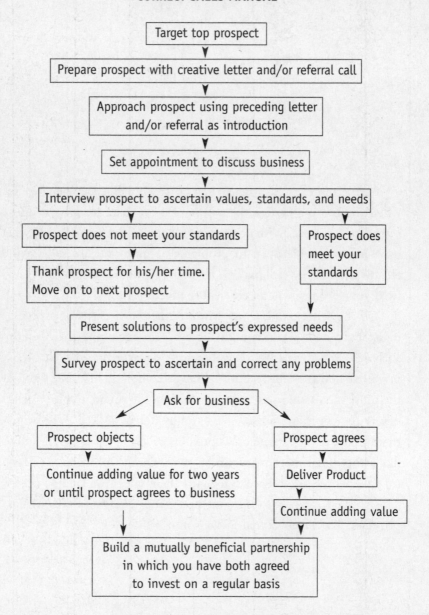

Target top prospect

↓

Prepare prospect with creative letter and/or referral call

↓

Approach prospect using preceding letter and/or referral as introduction

↓

Set appointment to discuss business

↓

Interview prospect to ascertain values, standards, and needs

↓   ↓

Prospect does not meet your standards   Prospect does meet your standards

↓

Thank prospect for his/her time. Move on to next prospect

Present solutions to prospect's expressed needs

↓

Survey prospect to ascertain and correct any problems

↓

Ask for business

↙   ↘

Prospect objects   Prospect agrees

↓   ↓

Continue adding value for two years or until prospect agrees to business   Deliver Product

↓

Continue adding value

↓

Build a mutually beneficial partnership in which you have both agreed to invest on a regular basis

With the correct mental sales manual, you can not only ensure that sales are solidified in the most efficient and effective manner, but you can also pinpoint any problems that arise. And let's face it; in the sales profession you will make mistakes. That's a given. But when you comprehend what it takes to construct a sale the right way—when you consistently consult the proper sales manual—you're also able to comprehend when, where, and why a mistake is made. That's because you have a standard to which you can constantly compare your selling efforts.

It's the same principle that many sports psychologists utilize when they recommend to their athlete-patients that they visualize themselves making the perfect putt or the perfect free throw or the perfect pass in order to improve their game. It's also the same reason so many top athletes regularly watch their top performances on video—because they understand that when they have a mental standard to uphold, it's easier to pinpoint their mistakes, and it's much easier to get back on track and stay there.

We'll address the main aspects of the proper sales manual in the upcoming chapters.[2] But for now, let's make sure that you clearly understand how the correct frame of reference in selling can put an end to tinkering in your sales career, if you are willing to make it your own.

A friend shared with me a story that will help drive this point home. While talking with a man whose job is tracking and seizing counterfeit money for the police department, my friend became intrigued to know how one trained for such a position. "You must have to study a lot of counterfeit bills to know one when you see one," he presumed. "No," the man replied. "We just get to know real bills like the backs of our hands. That way it becomes very easy to spot a counterfeit bill—regardless of what it looks like." And in similar fashion, avoiding the mistake of tinkering occurs when you know—like the back of your hand—what a solid, successful sale looks like from beginning to end, and then are able to hold that up as your standard of success. That way you will immediately know when, where, and why a problem occurred. And subsequently fixing a problem is just a matter of adjusting your efforts to reflect your selling standard.

SETTING YOUR STANDARD AND STICKING TO IT

When it comes down to it, knowing how to effectively remedy your sales problems plays a major role in determining the longevity of your sales career. The less time you spend tinkering around, the more time you will have to produce successful sales. In other words, the shorter and smaller your problems are, the longer and larger your career will be. Sure, problems will still arise when you have set and studied your standard of selling success. But believe me, when you've seen and then experienced a flawless sale, you'll want to strive for it every time. And when meeting your standard of selling success has become routine, you will know how to fix a problem the first time—even though it's the biggest one you've come across. One major player in the pharmaceutical industry demonstrated this in a refined fashion.

> **The less time you spend tinkering around, the more time you will have to produce successful sales.**

56

In the fall of 1982, pharmaceutical giant Johnson & Johnson was confronted with arguably the biggest crisis in the history of the pharmaceutical industry when seven people on Chicago's West Side mysteriously died. On a hunch from a couple of off-duty firemen, authorities quickly verified that each of the seven victims had ingested at least one Extra-Strength Tylenol capsule—Johnson & Johnson's best-selling product. When further tests were completed, it was revealed that each of the capsules in question was laced with 65 milligrams of cyanide, approximately 10,000 times more poison than is necessary to kill a human. Death for the victims was a certainty. But who was to blame?

News of the laced Tylenol capsules traveled quickly and caused a nationwide panic. The three national television networks warned viewers about the contaminated product, and the FDA advised consumers to avoid all Tylenol products until the source of the poisonings could be determined. As a result, people across the nation admitted themselves to hospitals for fear of having ingested laced Tylenol—and many more threw out their bottles in justifiable apprehension.

Obviously Johnson & Johnson had a major problem on its hands. Not only was consumer trust in its most profitable product bottoming out on a national scale, but consumer trust in the company as a whole was waning. Something had to be done—and fast. So Johnson & Johnson approached the biggest problem in its history as every sales professional should. The company immediately went to the root—knowing that it was the only hope to survive.

First on Johnson & Johnson's agenda was consumer safety. Instead of worrying about profits, as the Bayer Corporation did in its crisis, Johnson & Johnson worried about people, understanding that without consumers' trust, its products meant nothing. Without hesitation, the company alerted consumers across the nation to no longer consume or purchase any type of Tylenol product until the nature of the tampering could be ascertained. Furthermore, Johnson & Johnson executed a massive recall of all Tylenol capsules from the shelves of stores and warehouses, which included some 31 million bottles with a retail value of approximately $100 million. And to top it off, Johnson & Johnson posted a $100,000 reward for the killer and offered to exchange all Tylenol capsules that consumers had already purchased for Tylenol tablets.

The company knew these steps would cost it millions in losses, but the decision makers also knew it was a necessity if the problem was to be fixed immediately and thoroughly. Johnson & Johnson wanted to make it clear from the outset that it wasn't going to tinker around with the problem; and consequently its efforts to fix the problem continued until the issue was resolved and consumer trust was restored.

The recall of some 31 million bottles of Extra-Strength Tylenol was followed up by a consumer-first repackaging strategy. In an effort to assuage consumer worry, Johnson & Johnson reintroduced Extra-Strength Tylenol a few weeks later in new, tamper-resistant packaging, which included glued box flaps, a sealed bottle cap, and a foil seal atop the bottle opening with a warning on the label that cautioned: "Do not use if safety seals are broken." The packaging made Johnson & Johnson the first company in the pharmaceutical industry to utilize such strict safety guidelines. But the pharmaceutical giant didn't stop there. In addition to the new tamper-resistant packaging, Johnson & Johnson offered $2.50-off coupons on a national scale and implemented a new pricing program that gave additional discounts on Tylenol. It pulled out all the stops to solve the problem and ensure it wouldn't happen again.

Despite many naysayers, Johnson & Johnson believed its actions in dealing with the massive problem would eventually regain consumers' trust not only in the company name but also in Tylenol itself. And the company was right. When Johnson & Johnson sent out a large sales staff to reintroduce Tylenol to the medical community, the response was overwhelmingly positive. People felt safe knowing the company was looking out for their safety first. That was in 1983.

Today, twenty years later, Johnson & Johnson's Tylenol still reigns supreme by a wide margin. And there's no doubt that its level of supremacy has remained as a result of how Johnson & Johnson dealt with one very big problem. In fact, its succinct approach to a potentially disastrous problem was the very catalyst that kept Johnson & Johnson and its number-one product alive.

Like Johnson & Johnson, to avoid tinkering altogether, you must have a clear understanding of what ingredients go into making a successful sale—something Johnson & Johnson's previous success clearly indicated—and you must get at the root of any problem immediately and thoroughly. Johnson & Johnson did this despite the negative financial implications and potential fallout, and the company is still riding high. Bayer failed to do this, and the company is still paying for it. And so will you if you don't change your ways.

When you think about all the problems that can arise from a career in sales, it's fairly easy to see why tinkering is such a common mistake in the lives of busy, assertive, ambitious, don't-take-no-for-an-answer salespeople. And sometimes tinkering is an honest mistake. It's merely pit-stopping in an effort to stay in the race. But the truth is that when the smoke starts to clear (and I hope it's beginning to now), it's much easier to see how a sales career void of the fatal mistake of tinkering has a much longer, more prosperous life. In the end, that's the remedy that we're all seeking.

CHAPTER FOUR

Mistake #4: Moonlighting

*Building a business-based life instead
of a life-based business*

Prior to August 6, 2000, the term *forced overtime* was not a hot topic. In fact, it probably wouldn't have registered any results in a search of the article archives of the top newspapers and news magazines. But when some 87,000 employees of Verizon Communications went on strike that day against the nation's largest provider of local telephone and wireless services, many people perked up their ears.

Verizon is a communications giant in the United States. At the time of the strike the company had nearly 65 million access lines in 33 million households in 32 states, as well as 25 million wireless customers in all 50 states. In addition, the company had approximately 260,000 employees. While the numbers equaled big profits for the communications company, they also equaled big problems when one-third of its employees formed a multi-state picket line. And of all the factors that led to their protest, forced overtime was at the top of their list. One employee described the striking workers' concerns this way: "The company expects us to be at their beck and call and everything else be damned. I fully recognize that the company can't staff for the busiest day of the year and have people waiting around the rest of the time . . . But they've mismanaged the business because they don't staff adequately; they're dragging their feet hiring more employees. All we're asking is to have some control over our lives."[i]

As the story began to flood the airwaves, it became apparent that Verizon had been requiring many of its employees to accept overtime each week without forewarning. According to one report, "In New England management [could] force workers to work 10 hours a week in overtime and 12 hours during some months of the year. In Pennsylvania management [could] force workers to work 15 hours a week in overtime during five months of the year, and 10 hours during the remaining seven. In New Jersey there [was] no cap on the amount of overtime that [could] be imposed on workers."[2]

According to the same report, Verizon contended that the overtime was necessary to meet customer demands for services in a tight labor market. "We agree that work in our call centers is tough," said Eric Rabe a spokesperson for Verizon. "The question is: How can we address legitimate issues of job stress and still provide the service that customers want and deserve?" It was a legitimate concern. But was the answer more hours from existing employees? The employees didn't think so. Maybe the truth was that Verizon had fallen victim to its own faulty philosophy of productivity?

Verizon, it seemed, had built its mighty empire on the notion that working must come before living if one is to be successful. But the telecom giant found out the hard way that increasing employee hours on the job is *not* the fast track to more success. In fact, by the time Verizon finally reached tentative agreements with most of its employees on August 21, the [company] faced a backlog of 280,000 repair and installation orders."[3] In the end, the strike had affected the service of an estimated 25 million customers throughout twelve states and Washington, D.C.

A POTENTIALLY FATAL FASHION CONCEPT

Unfortunately Verizon's notion of sales productivity is not new to the sales industry. Across the country, people are working more hours in an effort to improve their job effectiveness. Blue Cross Consumer Health Interactive© contributor Loren Stein reported that "according to the Economic Policy Institute's 'State of Working America 2000–01,' in 1998 the typical middle-income, married-couple family worked six more weeks per year than a similar family in 1989. Furthermore, compared to 1969, such families in 1998 worked 14 more weeks per year."[4]

In 1998 the typical middle-income, married-couple
family worked six more weeks per year than
a similar family in 1989.

Workaholism has become chic in the last decade. It may very well be the prevalent banner of the sales profession. We tend to admire—even envy—the hard-working, long-hour-laboring, late-night-lingering salesperson who just seems to have the extra something that's required to succeed. Consider, for example, the approving write-up on Olympus Group (now Twin-Soft) CEO Julie Holdren in the September 2000 issue of *Washington Business Forward* magazine. According to columnist Stacey Schultz in an article titled, "And Baby Makes CEO," Holdren is due praise for the way she managed to fit her pregnancy into the busyness of her work schedule. And many join in Schultz's commendation.

As Schultz puts it, Julie Holdren gave birth to her first "baby," Olympus Group, in 1995 as a recent college graduate with $5,000 in her pocket. Back then, one-hundred-hour workweeks were common in an effort to sell not only the technology her company offered but also the company's name to its investors and eventual clients. Four years later, the company's success had allowed her to scale back to sixty- to seventy-hour workweeks. But when Holdren and her husband discovered she was pregnant, she determined to keep it a secret for six months until she decided how she would go about her pregnancy while simultaneously maintaining her busy schedule.

According to Schultz, Holdren deserves kudos for setting the tone of how her employees are expected to respond to pregnancies when there are deals to be made and work to be done. The writing of Holdren's employee "rulebook," as Schultz calls it, got under way when she worked up until the day before she gave birth to twin girls. A few more rules were written when she began making phone calls to her COO and attorney while lying in a hospital bed in the beginning stages of labor, citing that "negotiations were time sensitive." And when she conducted a staff conference call the day after giving birth, the ground rules were seemingly written in stone: when there is money to be made, when there are deals on the table, work comes first.

Professionals like Julie Holdren have become commonplace in the world of sales. We admire them for their relentless "work ethic." Whether one is selling technology or Toyotas, it has become very hip to work late nights and long hours—over weekends and through pregnancies—all in an effort to, at best, be successful and, at least, look successful. But what the purveyors of fashionable work trends don't tell you is that workaholism, like any addiction, can destroy your life in more ways than one. And maybe you've experienced this firsthand.

Late, lonely nights at the office lead to short, sleepless nights at home. Long, busy days on the job lead to lazy, careless health habits.

Frustrating, after-hours encounters with prospects lead to short tempers with friends. Lost relationships with clients lead to broken relationships with loved ones.

Yes, it takes time for workaholism to exact its toll. It takes time for the sales profession to become a burden on your life. It takes time for selling to spill over into living. But it happens—more often than we'd like to admit. And when it does, its effects can range from demoralizing to downright devastating. That's why the mistake I call "moonlighting" is the fourth fatal mistake of salespeople.

BURNING MORE THAN THE MIDNIGHT OIL

Moonlighting is a term we usually use to describe the act of working more than one job. As the term suggests, that second job usually takes place after business hours, under the "light of the moon." But in the sales profession, moonlighting is not simply the act of working extra hours; it's the belief that working more hours will lead to more success. It's thinking that to be successful, you must put in your time—sixty, seventy, eighty, and like Julie Holdren, even one hundred hours a week. It's the belief that working before the sun comes up and after the sun goes down is the way to success in the sales profession. But such thinking can destroy your life on and off the job. And the evidence is widespread.

In her article on forced labor, Blue Cross medical advisor Loren Stein also reported the following:

Recent research confirms that job stress related to overwork can translate into health problems and [serious] injuries. A 1999 Canadian study of long work hours found increased depression in workers, including unhealthy weight gain in men and drinking in women. Japanese workers, who are working longer and longer hours, have seen an increase in cardiovascular problems over the last five years. And a 1998 German study found that workers experienced a significant rise in accidents and traumatic incidents after 9 to 10 hours on a shift. Here in the United States, one such accident recently made headlines when Brent Churchill, a lineman for Central Maine Power, had to work back-to-back shifts all weekend with only a few hours sleep. Exhausted, Churchill was killed when he forgot to put on his insulating gloves before reaching for a 7,200-volt cable.[5]

Sure, moonlighting is usually born of ambition, which isn't inherently a bad thing. In fact, workaholism has often been called "the pretty addiction" because others often esteem the workaholic. But sometimes what began as a strategic short-term campaign to boost a business often ends up as a long-term custom of late nights, little sleep, and improper priorities.

The negative effects of moonlighting have been well researched and documented over the past few years and include such physical ailments as stress, high blood pressure, ulcers, chronic fatigue, migraines, and increased risk of heart disease. Not to mention the added stress it puts on relationships with your family and friends. In a groundbreaking study of families of workaholic fathers, family therapist Bryan Robinson found that the workaholic's high level of anxiety and depression is passed to his children, thus increasing the likelihood that they will also become workaholics or suffer from another form of lifestyle addiction. "Each family member," he writes, "gets drawn into the act [of workaholism] by waltzing around the workaholic's schedule, moods, and actions . . . [And] as workaholics dig their heels in and work longer and harder, their spouses, not unlike alcoholic spouses, often become consumed with trying to get them to curb their compulsive behaviors and spend more time in the relationship."[6]

Now, I realize that every salesperson has a long day here and a late night there; and that's not what moonlighting is about. The mistake of moonlighting occurs when your office becomes your dining room, living room, and bedroom all in one *because you believe it must be that way to be successful.* And when that happens, the results usually aren't pretty. Ultimately, in an effort to climb the so-called ladder of sales success, you end up burning a lot more than the midnight oil. And unfortunately, as PopPolitics.com contributor Karen Johnson points out, many companies in the sales industry have become very accommodating:

> Employees who are provided with food, exercise equipment and even showers at the office have fewer reasons to leave. . . .
>
> Busy employees may even be tempted to take advantage of comfortable couches rather than sleep at home when their schedules demand that they work late and arrive early. Certainly, bonuses, on-site fitness centers, cafeterias and Starbucks coffee in the kitchen are all wonderful advantages. However, after taking into account decreased family and leisure time and factoring in the amount that one's hourly rate decreases when the salary is divided by the amount of hours spent at work, in the end it may be more satisfying to leave work on time, go out for dinner and join your own gym.[7]

The promotion of longer hours at the office has not been beneficial to the sales masses. While some salespeople are able to make good use of the perks that Johnson's article mentions, in an effort to get out of the office earlier, most salespeople use the convenience of such amenities as a license to make their offices their homes. And in fact, that just might be what companies want. After all, more hours at the office mean more productivity, right? Not necessarily, as Johnson points out:

> In many ways work is good for us. It benefits our personal growth and intellect. But the benefits to body, mind and soul do not necessarily correspond with the number of hours worked. Medical reports released throughout the past decade show how detrimental overworking can be. In addition to the fatigue and stress caused by long hours, overworked employees can experience moderate to severe medical problems. They have less time to exercise, are more likely to skip doctor visits and tend to eat a less healthy diet. They are also more prone to both depression and suicide . . .
>
> Overworking damages personal lives as well. Working late robs people of valuable time to spend with their family, friends and themselves. The effect can also have negative consequences for the company. Health and personal problems associated with over-working can lead to increased sick days and less productivity.

To close her article, Johnson suggests that "as the New Economy increasingly enables us to connect to work at any time of the day or night, the need to learn how to disconnect has never been more urgent." And I couldn't agree more. The biggest farce in the sales industry is that more hours automatically mean more success and, therefore, a better life. Buying into the notion that working more will make you more successful and satisfied is like believing that eating more will make you more healthy and confident. *More* isn't the operative word in either case.

THE TRADE-OFF

I understand that for many salespeople moonlighting seems to be a necessity—it did for me, too, for several years. As salespeople, many of us are taught to believe that it's just what you have to do in order to be successful. And with a Puritan work ethic still lingering heavily in American society, moonlighting is rarely seen as an addiction—especially to those who suffer from it. But nevertheless, we still hear more sales sob stories than success stories when moonlighting becomes routine—maybe from our own mouths.

"Sorry I haven't called you in a while; things have been a little crazy at the office."

"I'm so sorry for missing your birthday. I feel awful. I've been working so much that it just slipped my mind."

"I'm sorry, honey. I won't be able to make it tonight. Tell the kids I love them and I'm very sorry. Tell them I'll make it up to them this weekend."

"Sorry I've been so distant. I guess that things just aren't working out as we planned. With this job, I just don't know if I can give you what you need."

The moonlighting story doesn't change that much over the years. What starts with an ambitious conviction ends up as a damaging addiction. Lengthy days linger into lazy nights. Long hours lead to shallow relationships. Late nights lead to mixed-up priorities and messed-up marriages. And the list goes on. You probably don't have to leave your company's building in order to witness the effects of moonlighting. The mayhem of moonlighting is everywhere you look in the sales profession, and you'd think that after all the bad press, salespeople would do something different. But most don't. Most just follow the same path, thinking that somehow they will not be like the others, thinking that somehow they will be immune to the consequences of moonlighting. But it doesn't happen. And the story of success-found-but-life-lost is written again and again . . . and maybe it's currently an autobiography.

Yes, it's very easy to fall prey to the mistake of moonlighting because the idea that you can actually be productive on the job *and* still have time to invest in the things you love off the job is a farce to most salespeople. "It's a nice thought, but it's not reality," many would say. "It takes a lot of blood, sweat, and tears to get to the top of the sales profession," most claim. And so, many salespeople have just accepted that the price to pay for sales success is life sacrifice.

But is it really worth it?

I mean that. Are the things you give up for the potential of more sales success really necessary trades? Consider some of the valuables that salespeople notoriously sacrifice in a push to reach the top. Then ask yourself: *Is what I potentially receive really worth the sacrifice?*

SACRIFICE	POTENTIALLY RECEIVE
Close friendships	Coworker rapport
Vacations	More time to sell
Health	Higher positions
Intimacy with family	Increased client base
Dreams	Dollars
Life satisfaction	Sales success

When you look at things that way, it's a little easier to see why the mistake of moonlighting can be so devastating. Moonlighting in any form is essentially the belief that more business means more life. It's building your life around your business instead of your business around your life. It's making selling your first priority by the actions you take and the time investments you make. *But the thing you end up selling the most is your soul.*

If we're really honest with ourselves, I doubt any of us would willingly trade the life we ultimately desire for more business. And I'm certain that you would not rather be sitting in your office for hours upon end than enjoying your relationship with the one you love most or basking in the light of your child's smile or laughing with close friends. But in more than two decades of selling and sales training, I've seen more salespeople make those trade-offs than I could ever count. I've seen salespeople sacrifice their health to pursue success—all the while thinking that it's just the price they must pay. I've seen salespeople miss family vacations to make more sales—all the while thinking it's just a necessary evil of the sales profession. I've seen salespeople lose their loves to get a leg up in their jobs—all the while thinking it was their spouses who wouldn't support them. And I've seen salespeople lose their very lives—figuratively and literally—under the guise of successful selling pursuits. I've seen more collateral sales damage than you can imagine. And that's because, whether we admit it or not, most salespeople believe that sales success somehow requires life sacrifice. But it's really the other way around. The truth is that to be successful in life, you must make sacrifices at work.

Ultimately being successful in any endeavor is a matter of keeping your priorities. And when your priorities in life are in order, the so-called necessity of moonlighting begins to fade. In American society we tend to separate business and life. When we're working, "business before pleasure" and "don't mix business and pleasure" are our common mantras. But I'm here to tell you that *business should not be separate from pleasure—in fact, it should be part of and party to pleasure.*

Please understand that I'm not making a claim that to do away with a moonlighting mentality, we should all go to work wearing our pajamas and slippers and pause for pizza and Ping-Pong every hour. I'm also not making a claim that salespeople need to lighten up about their jobs or that sales companies need to sponsor more team-building exercises, corporate matinees, and fun field trips. This isn't elementary school. We're all adults, and the sales industry is a grown-up job where grown-up decisions must be made to succeed. But I *am* saying that every salesperson needs to do away with the notion that business and pleasure—selling and living—are two separate things. Selling and living must complement each other if a salesperson is to be successful.

> Do away with the notion that business and pleasure—
> selling and living—are two separate things. Selling
> and living must complement each other.

The mistake of moonlighting begins with a mistaken ideology—and maybe that's where you went wrong. Moonlighting begins with the idea that business and life are two separate entities, and that part of being successful means keeping them separate. But in my twenty-three years of professional sales experience, I can say without reservation that I have never met a person who has lived by that creed and remained happy and satisfied. The fact is that you cannot shove life out your office window and achieve true success and satisfaction. Sure, you may get rich. You may win sales awards. But if you're like most, in the process you'll trade away the life you really love. That's because becoming a successful salesperson has everything to do with being a satisfied person.

Recently people from the *Denver Business Journal* asked me to speak at their annual Book of Lists conference, which gathers business leaders from more than sixty of the most dynamic markets in the United States. As I was leading the audience through some opening comments, I asked them, "How many of you would like your salespeople to achieve maximum productivity on the job?" As you might imagine, every hand went up. I then shared this thought with them: "For your employees to be productive on the job, they must have a standard of success *off* the job." I have never seen so many people take notes at one time. I went on to share with them the following thoughts.

Success in sales has everything to do with keeping personal priorities. In other words, salespeople can increase their success only by putting boundaries on their businesses that help them uphold and promote their priorities throughout the day. *If you don't put boundaries on your business, you'll never achieve balance in your life.* Success by definition is supposed to produce satisfaction. Therefore, your sales career, if it is successful, should produce more life satisfaction. But if you don't know what makes you a satisfied person in the first place, you'll frequently invest time in things that don't matter and strive for things that don't add to your fulfillment in life.

If there is an auxiliary definition for the mistake of moonlighting, it would be this: working harder for things that don't really matter . . . spinning your wheels at full speed . . . seeking a pseudo-success that has nothing to do with your priorities in life. And foundationally that's a result of not knowing what you're working for—not knowing what is most important in life to you—and not having any boundaries on your business to promote those things.

On the other hand, when you know what you value, when you

can articulate what a fulfilling life really looks like, then you have a clear standard of success for which to strive. And with your standard of success, you are able to determine whether you are truly being productive with your selling efforts (promoting life fulfillment) or being unproductive with your selling efforts (promoting things that don't matter in the end).

Before we move on to the next chapter, you need to be clear on the nonnegotiables in your life—your priorities that shape your standard of success. That's because ultimately your priorities are foundational to avoiding the fatal mistake of moonlighting, and they are fundamental to avoiding the next mistake we will discuss.

The following is a very simple strategy for aligning your life priorities with your notion of sales success. In an effort to help you avoid the mistake of moonlighting once and for all, I will take you through four steps so that you may construct a proper standard of success for your sales business. And once you have this in place, its purpose is to become a constant reminder—an accountability partner of sorts—by which you can readily gauge how truly successful you are each day. If this is something you haven't ever done or haven't done in a while, I encourage you to take your time completing this exercise. It is integral to your long-term success as a sales professional and ultimate satisfaction as a person. Here we go.

Your first step is to write down the top ten things that are important to you in life (for example, health, family, financial security, traveling, and so forth). Don't worry about any particular order at this point. Just write them as they come to mind. The only stipulation is that you cannot list more or less than ten. With this step you are merely clarifying your priorities. This may prove to be fairly easy if you completed the "Ahead to 80" exercise in the first chapter.

If you'd like to have a separate copy of the following exercises, please visit www.killingthesale.com.

1.

2.

3.

4.

5.

6.

7.

8.

9.

10.

For the next step, rank your top five priorities in the following space, the highest priority at the top, the lowest priority at the bottom. This step may be a little more difficult because it requires you to pit one priority against another and remove items from the list that are not the *most* important. However, this step is necessary because I have found most salespeople who complete this exercise end up with a few items on their list that are not really "top" priorities when compared to others. This step is intended to weed out anything that is not of *utmost* importance, and most people can quantify their nonnegotiable priorities with five items. We'll talk about the Vision Statement and Mission Statements parts shortly.

1. Priority:

   Vision statement:

   Mission statement:

2. Priority:

   Vision statement:

   Mission statement:

3. Priority:

   Vision statement:

   Mission statement:

4. Priority:

   Vision statement:

   Mission statement:

5. Priority:

   Vision statement:

   Mission statement:

For the third step, below each priority on your list, write a vision statement in present tense that indicates the ideal embodiment of that priority. For example, if health is one of my top five priorities, I'd write, "By preserving and strengthening my body, I maximize my energy throughout the day and am able to keep my other priorities more consistently." If I were writing a vision statement about my family, I'd write, "By upholding my family as a higher priority than my work, I show them that they are the most important people in my life and therefore alleviate any doubt in their minds that I love them with all my heart."

For the last step, compose a mission statement that indicates how you plan to uphold each priority as a sales professional. For example, if I again were to use health as one of my top priorities, I'd write something like: "I will exercise for at least forty-five minutes a day, no less than five times a week. I will maintain a healthy diet by refusing snacks, avoiding fast food, drinking plenty of water, and planning meals ahead of time. I will not schedule meetings that cause conflict with these commitments, nor will I bend the rules for the sake of customer or coworker approval." If family was one of my top priorities, I'd write something like: "I am a faithful and loving husband to my wife. I will not sacrifice quality time with her for a customer or coworker. I am also a supportive and encouraging father. I will not trade quality time with my boys for the sake of sales success. Furthermore, I will not place work events above their sporting events or school events. I will not waste time during the workday so that I am always able to leave the office no later than 5:00 P.M. to spend the evening with my family. I will not work weekends unless my wife and boys have prior engagements in which I am not involved."

As you can begin to see, although such statements are not necessarily related to *how* you should sell, they are the standard of what your selling efforts should promote and produce. In other words, to be truly successful, your daily selling efforts must support and supplement each statement that you have written.

Once you've completed this exercise, tear out the page and keep it near you—on your desk, on the wall in your office, or on your mirror at home. You may even want to give a copy of your list to an accountability partner who has permission to ask you at any time how you are doing with living out your mission statements, with maintaining your standard of success.

Whatever you decide to do with your list, make sure that you review it on a regular basis. Will you still have unsuccessful days? Yes. You're not perfect. You will mix up your priorities now and then. But the longer you hold to your standard of success, the more naturally it will become for you to say no when you need to say no, and yes when you need to say yes. Similarly with a constant reminder of your personal, priority-centered standard of success, you will find yourself consciously motivated to rid your days of unproductive activities so that you consistently meet your standard. (More on this is in the next chapter.)

Essentially, your five mission statements will embody your clearest and highest definition of success. When your selling efforts meet your standards, you can rest assured that you are walking the path of your most successful, satisfying life. Of course, you can complete this exercise and then act contrary to your priorities—and you'll still end up walking a moonlit path and eventually suffering the consequences. Truth be told, that's your prerogative. You've probably written goals or standards or priorities before, and then not done anything with them. And you can do that now. It's your life to lose. But if you've been inspired to eliminate the mistake of moonlighting from your sales career, this is where you must start. (Next chapter, we will discuss how to clean up your sales practices, which will make it much easier to uphold your priorities while remaining productive.)

What you must understand at this point is that the success paradigm all great sales professionals follow is this: *selling is what you do in the process of living.* It's not the other way around. Life does not happen after work is done. Living is supposed to be supported and supplemented by selling. Therefore, you must adapt your selling endeavors to your most treasured life. That's why maintaining a successful sales strategy is founded on your ability to promote your life-centered priorities throughout the day—no matter what.

And if you still think it's not possible to be highly successful in sales *and* satisfied in life, think again. In *High Trust Selling,* I shared dozens of stories of salespeople who increased their levels of success not by increasing their hours on the job, but by *increasing* their awareness of their priorities and *decreasing* the time they spent on things that wouldn't promote the lives they desire. Essentially each one of them did away with the mistake of moonlighting, and the results speak for themselves: a decrease in time working, an increase in sales productivity, and an increase in quality of life. In case you missed that book, here are a few snapshots of some of those amazing before-and-after stories:

	BEFORE	AFTER
Jean Dees:	55 hours/week	30 hours/week
	Sales rep	President of company
	2 weeks of vacation/year	Unlimited vacation
Ian McDonald:	5–6 days/week	4 days/week
	$22 million in sales/year	$100 million in sales/year[8]
	1–2 weeks of vacation/year	Unlimited vacation

Tim Broadhurst:	30 clients	12 clients
	$10 million in sales/year	$80 million in sales/year
	1 week of vacation/year	15 weeks of vacation/year
Tom Ramirez:	80 hours/week	40 hours/week
	100 orders/month	300 orders/month[9]
	1 week of vacation/year	Unlimited vacation

These are only four of literally thousands of similar stories that I have witnessed over the years. And all are testimonies to what can happen when a moonlighting mentality is replaced with a life-focused paradigm of success. These stories and my company's two decades of research have revealed that when your priorities are clear in your life, it's much easier to be motivated to increase your per-hour productivity in your work. Putting life as your first priority causes you to look at your business differently. It inspires you to evaluate your client base: "Are all my clients profitable investments of my time and energy?" It inspires you to look at the hours you have in a day and make decisions that allow you to squeeze the juice out of each one of those hours: "Am I spending any time on meaningless, unproductive activities?" It inspires you to become a more efficient and professional salesperson who constantly asks, "Is there a better and more efficient way to do this?" In short, it inspires you to answer some critical questions on a regular basis, namely, "Is my business producing more of the life I desire?" And in the end, when you've created a life-centered standard of success, you have a solid foundation on which to base your selling efforts and increase your selling efficiency.

And that brings us to the subject of our next chapter.

CHAPTER FIVE

Mistake #5: Muscling

*Taking Lone Ranger actions instead of
using team-connected strategies*

I suppose it was my dad who first introduced me to the concept of muscling when I was still young. He understood how to avoid it. I, on the other hand, was only a boy, and I didn't understand things as he did. Like many salespeople, I had to learn things the hard way.

I must have been about ten years old when I spent some time at work with my dad one afternoon, observing his responsibilities as a doctor. I remember being fascinated by the idea of a giant camera taking X-ray pictures of people's insides—images a normal camera couldn't produce. I imagine that at the time I was quite influenced by what I saw on television and read in books. X-ray vision was, of course, a necessary skill that every superhero must have if he was good for anything. And the thought that my father had access to "X-ray vision" technology was thrilling to me. The only problem was that he was a radiologist, not an X-ray technician. In other words, he was the one who read the X-rays, but he didn't take them.

Puzzled, I asked, "Dad, why don't you take the pictures?" *Surely,* I thought, *he would want to take advantage of such an extraordinary skill.*

"Son," he replied, "I get paid to *read* the X rays."

It was a very significant point to consider. It's too bad his wisdom didn't readily sink in back then. If I had been a little older and little wiser, I might have saved myself quite a bit of frustration and failure in my selling career.

THE LEADING CAUSE OF SALES ATROPHY

Whether or not he knew it, my dad's response that day indicated that he was very clear about his on-the-job responsibilities. My father knew that as a radiologist certain tasks were productive, and others were not—even if they could be viewed as part of the radiology process. In short, he understood his job description. Something many salespeople don't seem to readily comprehend . . . until it's too late. Until they're a salesperson, secretary, assistant, courier, copier, filer, faxer, computer-repair technician, and social-activities director all in one. Until their sales job is no longer a job for one salesperson; it's a job for ten people—the only problem is that it's still being carried out by one very weary salesperson. Have you ever felt overwhelmed with your "responsibilities"? Have you ever looked at your workweek on Monday and wondered how in the world you were going to get everything done? Have you ever felt like your job is more than you can handle? A client and good friend of mine named Linda Davidson once felt that way.

When Linda returned from one of our events, she knew she was caught up in a whirlwind of responsibilities. She was not only a busy salesperson, she was her own assistant, secretary, office manager, marketing rep, and database manager—and she was suffering under the weight of responsibility. But she wasn't the only one suffering. Her clients were not getting her full attention, and therefore she was not receiving their full business. As a result, she was having to work harder than necessary to close sales. All in all, that was making Linda's sales job feel more like a burden than a blessing. And that didn't sit right. She knew she loved building relationships with clients, and she knew she wanted to continue. But to realize her potential and give her clients the attention they deserved, she realized that something needed to change.

The first thing Linda did was begin tallying the time she spent on different tasks throughout her days. That may seem trivial to you. But for her it was just what the doctor ordered. After she tallied up the results of one week, it was clear to Linda why she was feeling so overwhelmed. The numbers spoke for themselves:

TASK	TIME SPENT PER WEEK
Copying	5 hours
Faxing	4 hours
Emailing	5 hours
Talking on the phone*	20 hours

* Phone calls that are unnecessary/non-sales calls or status calls

Total Time spent each week	34 hours

In short, Linda was working hard, but she wasn't working smart. She was spending time becoming somewhat successful, instead of investing time and reaping a full harvest. Ultimately, she had fallen victim to the fifth fatal mistake salespeople make: something I call "muscling."

A POTENTIALLY FATAL FATIGUE

Muscling is a sister to the mistake of moonlighting. It, too, is a common mistake of an ambitious, super-salesperson. However, muscling is distinct from the mistake of moonlighting and therefore requires a treatment of its own.

As you learned in the previous chapter, the mistake of moon-lighting is based on mistaken ideology (an improper standard of sell-ing success) and therefore requires a change in philosophy in order to stop (a new standard of selling success that takes into account your top priorities in life). Muscling, on the other hand, is based on mistaken behavior (an improper strategy of productivity) and there-fore requires a change in selling practice. In other words, whereas moonlighting begins in your thinking, muscling could be described as simply not thinking at all or just doing whatever is on your plate. Something I was guilty of in the not-too-distant past.

About three years ago, I was my company's president, opera-tions manager, accountant, personnel manager, marketing manager, writer, and speaker—and the company was growing at a modest rate of 2.5 percent per year. Now, I am just the full-time speaker, and the company is growing at a rate of 46 percent per year. Clearly when I was doing everything, I was not nearly as productive as I could or should have been.

Even when you have a priority-centered standard of success in mind as I do, your selling days can still get out of hand. You can still be tremendously unproductive. That's because changing your para-digm of success is only half the battle. To truly begin to reap the life you most desire from your selling efforts, you must do more than merely work hard with the limited time you allot yourself each day. Unfortunately that's all many salespeople do.

Essentially muscling is overestimating the value of doing and underestimating the value of delegation. It's doing everything in the selling process yourself—whether it is necessary that *you* do it—and delegating nothing. *You've no doubt heard of multitasking.*

Muscling is multijobbing. And if left alone, the mistake of muscling will eventually lead to sales atrophy.

I often compare the consequences of muscling to something in the fitness world called "overtraining." Decades of studies have shown that although working out has obvious benefits to the health and appearance of one's body, many die-hard fitness enthusiasts often end up in an overambitious routine that begins to break down their muscles rather than build them up. Overtraining occurs when the muscles are constantly overworked and never given time to recover. If this state continues long enough, progress decreases, and the workout enthusiast eventually experiences loss of performance, loss of muscular strength, and loss of muscle mass. The creators of intense-workout.com describe overtraining this way:

> It's the number one reason most of the people in your gym look like they have never stepped into a gym before in their life. It's the reason most people don't see the gains they want, and give up right away. It's what you don't want to do . . . You can do the best exercises, with the best form for years, and still see no gains if you're doing too much.[1]

In an article titled "Muscle Injury and Overtraining," bodybuilding.com writer David Knowles cites the following symptoms of overtraining:

- Decrease in performance with increased effort
- Loss of body weight
- Chronic fatigue
- Elevated heart rate and blood pressure levels

- Psychological staleness

- Sleep disturbances

- Decreased appetite

- Muscle tenderness

- Occasional nausea

Do any of these symptoms sound familiar? Just as overtraining can seriously limit your fitness progress, the mistake of muscling can severely cut into your sales progress and profits. When muscling becomes your selling mode of operation, your selling muscles become increasingly fatigued, you find it hard to maintain your selling energy, and you eventually begin to break down your selling strength to the point of permanent depletion. And when that happens, it's very difficult to revive your selling stamina or maintain your emotional enthusiasm to continue selling. In fact, you could theoretically work only forty hours a week and still fall victim to muscling. That's because muscling is essentially having to try too hard in order to succeed in sales—whether that translates into having to complete thirty tasks over eight hours or fifty tasks over fifteen hours.

If you read my last book, *High Trust Selling*, you might remember a story I shared about a salesperson named Tom who at one time in his career was a study in muscling. He was putting in eighty-hour workweeks on a regular basis primarily because he was handling every task that came his way—productive or not—and delegating nothing. And truth be told, his wallet was getting buff. But when he ended up in the hospital with a brain aneurysm that required immediate surgery, he finally came to terms with the nearly fatal mistake he had been making. After leaving the hospital, he began delegating everything except what he loved doing—prospecting and selling—

and within a year his company's business doubled while his weekly hours on the job were cut in half. And the same can happen for you if you're willing to get down to business.

BUILDING UP OR BREAKING DOWN?

Think of muscling in this light. Different jobs have different responsibilities. A CPA's job is to manage finances and taxes. A lawyer's job is to preserve the legal rights of the client. Your job as a salesperson is to sell. And regardless of your product or service, a highly productive selling business *requires* you to take on only two responsibilities:

1. Building trust with the right prospects

2. Adding value to existing clients

That, as my dad would say, is what you get paid to do. When it comes down to it, these two responsibilities are the core of every successful sales business. If you can build trust with the right prospects and add value to existing clients well and often, you will succeed without question, as literally thousands of my clients like Linda Davidson have.[2]

If you remember, when we left Linda, she had discovered that she had been spending more than 50 percent of her time each day on tasks that could be delegated or removed from her day. Well, things didn't stay that way for long once she realized her mistake.

One by one, Linda delegated tasks to her team, who she quickly learned were just as capable, if not more capable than she was, to carry out the tasks. By her own admission, it was tough giving up control and responsibility. "But I realized," she says, "that I didn't have to be a superwoman with every task to succeed." With some relevant coaching help, she put an end to her self-titled "ego-thing" and began letting her team do what they do so well.[3] And you know what? When you look at the numbers, it's easy to see why Linda refers to that move as "the best business decision" she's ever made. Since delegating all tasks but her top responsibilities, Linda and her team have increased their business by 183 percent. Clearly Linda is not the only one happy with her new methods of productivity. Her clients are smiling too.

When it comes down to it, every necessary task that arises apart from your top two responsibilities as a salesperson can be delegated. Such action is necessary to truly build up your sales business instead of breaking it down (more on this in a minute). Your most productive responsibilities as a salesperson do not include filing or collating or faxing or answering every e-mail and phone call. Sure, they are necessary tasks of the selling process, but they are not highly productive and, therefore, should be given only a nominal time investment. However, many salespeople still spend hours every week on such tasks. Many salespeople are still trying to do it all. As a result, they're working much harder than necessary to sustain sales success. And like an overtraining fitness fanatic, they end up with results that are far short of their aspirations. They expected to experience noticeable growth; instead, they're worn out, disappointed with their results, and increasingly weary of selling. And if that's how you've been feeling, it's time to change your selling routine.

Now, I know what you might be thinking: *Then how am I supposed to do all the things that need to get done? How do I send faxes that need to be sent? How do I make copies that need to be made? How do I make sure calls and e-mails are answered?* And these are valid concerns. There are, without a doubt, many necessary tasks that come up in the process of setting prospects' expectations and meeting clients' needs, and the tasks must be completed. I recognize that there are certain calls you need to take and tasks you need to complete for friends and family—whether or not they have to do with selling. I understand that selling stirs up many tasks throughout the course of the day and living stirs up even more. They do in my own workday as well. I'm not suggesting that you simply ignore these tasks. But I *am* telling you that in order for you to do away with the mistake of muscling in your sales career—in order for you to avoid sales burnout—in order for your sales business to flourish—you need to spend as much time as possible on your top two selling responsibilities. And that will require delegating some tasks that have occupied your workdays.

DETERMINING TO DELEGATE

In the past, I've written and spoken extensively about your need to clean up the silly, wasteful tasks from your day as part of an effort to become more productive in selling. And that, of course, holds true in our discussion now. However, I am going to assume that you don't need me to explain why such escapism tasks as playing computer games, surfing the Web, gossiping with coworkers, and instant messaging with friends are highly unproductive and must be removed from your daily routine. Let's just say that if you expect to increase your selling productivity and hence your quality of life, that begins when you at least have the discipline to spend your working hours on work-related tasks.

I think you know what I mean.

Beyond that initial discipline, removing the mistake of muscling from your selling career begins when you take an honest inventory of how you are spending your time. Like Linda Davidson, you may need to literally track how you spend your time for a few days. Not only will this exercise open your eyes to the unproductive nature of muscling, but it will also inspire you to do something about it (which we will discuss in a minute).

There are many ways to take inventory of your time, but I've found that the most efficient way is to pause at the end of every working hour and record how you spent the four fifteen-minute increments that have just passed. Don't get bogged down with insignificant details when you're describing tasks. Just record the gist of how you spent each particular fifteen-minute increment, and do this for at least three working days. (I realize that this exercise will take time from your top two selling responsibilities, but it is a necessity if you are guilty of trying to muscle your way to success.)

For example, your morning inventory might look something like this:

Tuesday, February 2

9:00–9:15 A.M.:	Made coffee. Talked to coworkers.
9:15–9:30 A.M.:	Listened to phone messages. Reviewed calendar. Read e-mails.
9:30–9:45 A.M.:	Answered personal e-mails. Answered work e-mails. Updated calendar.
9:45–10:00 A.M.:	Confirmed lunch appointment. Talked to client who called regarding order status. Faxed order contract.
10:00–10:15 A.M.:	Updated calendar. Returned two clients' calls. Called a prospect.
10:15–10:30 A.M.:	Prepared for staff meeting. Talked to client who called regarding order status. Talked to prospect who returned call.

10:30–10:45 A.M.:	Sales staff meeting
10:45–11:00 A.M.:	Sales staff meeting
11:00–11:15 A.M.:	Listened to phone messages. Returned one client's call. Scheduled follow-up meetings with two clients. Talked to prospect who called with questions about product.
11:15–11:30 A.M.:	Returned one client's call. Followed up on order status for two clients.
11:30–11:45 A.M.:	Called two clients to give them confirmed order status. Filled out paperwork for one new client order. Made copies of paperwork. Sent confirmation of order to client.
11:45–12:00 P.M.:	Listened to phone messages. Filed paperwork for new order. Updated calendar. Prepared for lunch appointment with prospect. Drove to lunch appointment with prospect at noon.

Now, if that was the first half of *your* day, you may look at that inventory and think, *Well, at least I'm not completely wasting my time on things like computer games, personal e-mailing, and socializing.* And you'd have a good point. But, you see, making the mistake of muscling is not simply the act of wasting time; it's the act of spending time unproductively. It's doing everything instead of *just* the most productive things. And the truth is that if you tallied up the amount of time spent on the top two selling responsibilities in the example, you would find that only about 25 percent of the total time worked was spent on the most productive selling tasks. And in the dog-eat-dog world of sales, investing one of every four hours on your most productive responsibilities just won't cut it. Sure, you may be working hard and exercising a strong work ethic, but many other salespeople in your sales arena are doing the same thing—and those who are the most successful are the ones who are spending most, if not all, of their time on their top selling responsibilities.

If your days are very busy but you are not very successful, chances are good that you're suffering from the symptoms of muscling. But the good news is that when you begin to take steps to increase your productivity, when you begin to increase the time you invest in your top two selling responsibilities, both your success and the level of your sanity begin to increase as well. Let's discuss how to do this.

REVAMPING YOUR DAILY ROUTINE

To this point, we've established that you can't continually spend time on tasks that don't directly further your business and then expect your business to flourish. Like Linda Davidson, you have to realize that something needs to give in order for you to maximize the time spent on your top selling responsibilities. And for many salespeople, the tasks that need to go aren't all futile. They are often tasks that are necessary parts of your selling business, such as:

- Copying paperwork for customers

- Faxing information to customers

- Answering phones

- Answering e-mails

- Marketing products and services

- Scheduling appointments

Many tasks that musclers take on must continue to be completed. But if you're guilty of muscling, you need to understand that *you* don't need to do such tasks. In fact, the less time you spend on activities like those listed, the faster your business will flourish and the less time success will require. Consider how much time the average salesperson could free up every year by no longer performing such tasks[4]:

TASK	AVG. TIME SPENT PER DAY	TIME FREED UP PER YEAR IF DELEGATED
Copying	30 minutes	125 hours
Faxing	15 minutes	62.5 hours
E-mailing	60 minutes	250 hours
Answering phones	60 minutes	250 hours
Updating calendar	20 minutes	83.3 hours

Total time freed up per year: 770.8 hours, or 96 workdays

Can you imagine? If you found a way to delegate only those five tasks, you would have nearly ninety-six more eight-hour days to sell every year. Do you think you could increase your success if you had almost eight hundred more hours a year to sell? Furthermore, don't you think you could invest more time in your top life values if you had that much more time on your hands? The answers go without saying. It's difficult to see the negative effects of muscling on a small scale—one day at a time. But when you look at the bigger picture, things become much more clear. When you think about how much more time you could have to do the two things that would literally spur your success more than any other, it's not difficult to become motivated to make a change.

GIVING UP TO GET AHEAD

Contrary to what you may be thinking, I'm not going to suggest that to combat the mistake of muscling, you run out and spend your entire paycheck on hiring two assistants and a marketing firm. For most of us, it's not that easy. All of us don't have thousands of dollars put away for a rainy day or an ailing business. As with any investment, the initial amount invested and the level of risk are up to you—and by the way, the investment doesn't necessarily have to be monetary. But you have to start somewhere.

You need to adopt a "CEO mind-set" in order to make a wise investment into the future of your sales business. A CEO mind-set is looking at your sales business as you would your own company, then determining to make investments that will ensure your "company's" long-term stability. That may require a financial investment of your own money. That may require a business loan. Or that may require more self-discipline. The important thing to remember is to start off with an investment that you can afford, but make sure to stretch your investment. And then as you begin to reap more income, increase your delegation until you are eventually spending all of your time on your top two responsibilities.

There are many ways that you can do this. But once you have confirmed the main tasks that are sapping your selling time and strength, I recommend that you try one or more of the following creative ways to begin giving up your less-productive responsibilities in order to spend more time on your most-productive ones.

As you read through these six suggestions, please understand that your level of investment—financial or otherwise—is ultimately up to you. But generally speaking, the more you are willing to invest, the more quickly you are able to reap a return. To become comfortable with the idea of investing money or time to give up some of your less-productive responsibilities, determine how much money you could make per hour if you devoted all of your time to your top two productive activities, and then weigh that figure against any investments you might make. The results are generally lopsided in favor of making the investments.

1. HIRE YOURSELF.

I'm not kidding. If you are convinced that a little more self-discipline will keep you from making the mistake of muscling, then hire yourself for no more than two hours a day to take care of the less-productive-but-necessary tasks. Block an hour or two to spend solely on the tasks that you need to get done, but that are not your most productive. And make sure to block your hour(s) at periods during your workday when your top two selling responsibilities are least feasible. This may mean blocking your first hour of the day or your last hour, or even committing to eat your lunch in your office while you complete your less-productive tasks. But understand that taking this step is a commitment to work *only* on unproductive-but-necessary tasks during the time you specify and not at any other time. In other words, if your time to retrieve e-mail and voice mail is from 12:00 to 1:00 P.M. each day, then you won't return calls or answer e-mail during any other time.

When you've spent a few weeks working for yourself, three things will probably happen. First, you will get a very clear picture of a job description if and when you do decide to hire someone full- or part-time. Second, you will become much more disciplined to spend the remainder of your day either building trust with prospects or adding value to clients. Third, you will probably become more open to the option of delegation. Okay, so I tricked you a little bit.

The truth is that delegation is always the best option, but if you want to give this remedy a shot, more power to you. However, if you can't finish all your less-productive tasks in two hours, you need to seriously consider another option on this list.[5]

2. HIRE A RESPONSIBLE YOUNG PERSON YOU KNOW.

I'm sure you know of more than one teenager or college student who would be more than willing to spend a few hours a day taking less-productive tasks off your hands. Many salespeople could tremendously benefit from delegating a couple of hours a day of filing, copying, collating, and mailing. But make certain that if you go this route, you train the person thoroughly and have a good accountability system in place. Also, make sure the person is clear on the responsibilities and understands that asking you for confirmation on a task is always the best option to ensure it's done right the first time. Taking this step will require some faith on your part in order to release tasks that are not highly productive, but nevertheless important to your business. But if you're willing to take the time to train someone comprehensively, it will be worth your effort in the long run.

3. HIRE A COACH.

For many salespeople, this is the absolute first step to gaining more control of their selling time. Often, a fresh pair of eyes on your selling days can add insight to help you ascertain where you need to be spending the majority of your time. Furthermore, a coach will help you stay on track once you make decisions on how to—and how not to—invest your working hours. In short, a coach offers much-needed accountability to an otherwise difficult, individualistic discipline.[6] And remember that the key to making the most of a coaching relationship is to be honest and completely forthcoming about your struggles—especially if it's difficult for you to relinquish control of tasks that pertain to your work.

4. SHARE AN ASSISTANT WITH A COWORKER OR COLLEAGUE WHOSE VALUES YOU SHARE.

When you don't have the means to hire an assistant by yourself, why not go in with a coworker or colleague whom you trust and respect? If you share an assistant with a coworker, you cut the cost in half, and you share the training responsibility. This is obviously the best scenario because your assistant always remains in the same place. But if you don't have a coworker with whom you'd feel comfortable sharing an assistant, hire one with a trusted colleague at a nearby office or in another field altogether. A top-quality assistant may enjoy the regular change of environment and pace. If you go this route, it's important that you not tie your assistant's hands. When training a newly hired assistant, always allow for innovation and suggestions for improvement. The fact is that a great assistant will often be able to figure out more productive and creative methods for completing tasks—and your job is always to support that, not squash it.

5. LET YOUR ASSISTANT HIRE AN ASSISTANT.

In many cases, a sales professional's assistant is so overloaded with tasks that he or she can barely stay above water alone. And adding more tasks to that person's plate will probably result in burnout. In such scenarios, let your assistant hire an assistant. You'll end up with two assistants to whom you can delegate your least productive tasks. Now, I don't recommend this option to everyone. But if you are in a position where your sales volume is steadily increasing, take this step ahead of time in order to build your capacity to handle all the responsibilities that will arise from business growth. That way you will ensure that you won't be tempted to muscle when business starts booming.

6. PROMOTE YOUR ASSISTANT.

If you already have an assistant, but find that the two of you are still overwhelmed with tasks day in and day out, give your assistant a promotion. Don't ever presume that all your assistant can (or wants to) do is your "dirty work." If you have a responsible, sharp assistant, give that person more responsibility. Empower your assistant to help you prospect, follow up after sales, or even do some selling along with you. You may find that together, you can eliminate less-productive tasks from your day, and you may be able to produce a greater volume of business. And don't be surprised at how open your assistant may be to an opportunity to be more directly involved in the selling process.

THE PREMIUM SUPPLEMENT FOR STRONG SALES EFFORTS

All great salespeople need empowered teams to reach the peak of selling success—something a client named Harry Gordon learned before it was too late.

On his own admission, Harry used to run his sales business with the belief that he could do his work better than anyone else. He had surrounded himself with a team of people who simply took messages and tallied tasks for him—but they didn't return calls or carry out the tasks. Harry hadn't empowered them to do any of that. He *did* believe in taking care of each client, which wasn't a bad thing— but Harry *didn't* believe anyone else could do it like he did. As a result, his team's potential was untapped, and his clients weren't receiving the full measure of his attention and time. And his time, by the way, was adding up.

A typical week for Harry meant getting in early and working until approximately 7:00 P.M. with at least one weekend day of work in order to catch up. In short, Harry's muscles were being flexed—but when it came down to it, his business wasn't getting much bigger.

Harry was at his muscling peak in 1996 when at our multiple-day Sales Mastery™ event, he regularly positioned himself near the doors to ensure that he would be the first attendee to the pay phones during each break. He didn't like watching all the other attendees talking, laughing, and enjoying themselves. But he felt that to grow his business, spending every spare second on the phone was a necessity. He would, however, learn otherwise.

According to Harry, it was in a "blinding flash of the obvious" that his liberation came. As I shared with the audience the morbid truths of the mistake of muscling in a selling career, Harry realized that his muscling habits had put him on a fast track to selling atrophy. And he knew he needed to change.

When he returned home from the event, Harry immediately began determining what he could delegate in order to free up more time to sell. Shortly thereafter, he asked his team members to shadow him throughout the course of his day in order to learn every aspect of his job. And it wasn't long before all four of them could handle every task that might arise in a given day.

Today, "Team Gordon," as the four call themselves, runs the show. Harry is kept up-to-date on fulfillment progress with formal two-hour meetings every Monday. And that's smart. Harry doesn't want to be surprised by anything. But ultimately the success is up to the team; his part is building and fostering the relationships with clients—that's all. And that simple job description affords Harry a relatively stress-free forty-hour-a-week job that produced almost $100 million last year in sales, a 400 percent increase from his 1996 total. That's what I call maxing your potential without taxing your time and energy.

The fact is that in the selling profession, you cannot do it all alone, especially if you desire to maintain your priorities in life while sustaining a high degree of sales success. Delegation to the right people makes everything easier, not only on the job but also in your life. With delegation, not only are you given abundant opportunity to produce mega-amounts of sales, but you gain the peace of mind that comes from knowing you are not taking from one pile of responsibilities only to build up another pile. And when muscling is a thing of the past, the end of your workday is no longer a sigh of relief—it's a knowing smile of satisfaction.

CHAPTER SIX

Mistake #6: Arguing

*Selling your product before knowing
your customer*

When I spoke with my friend Mike a few years ago, I was
logging thousands of air miles a year. I was looking for one
company to handle all of my ongoing travel needs, and he knew the
owner of a rather successful travel agency. Following our conversation, Mike arranged a meeting between the owner and me.

As a consumer, I am always open to exploring new ways to maximize the value of money that I exchange for goods and services. In
this particular case, I was not only looking for new ways to stretch
my traveling dollars; I was also looking for innovative ways to
shrink my traveling time. When the owner and I sat down together,
I was eager to share with him some of my most important values
and needs in regard to traveling. I wanted him to know that being
home was more important than being on the road. I wanted him to
know that my family always takes precedence over my work; therefore, if I needed to spend more money to fly on a direct flight that
would give me more family time, I wouldn't hesitate. I was anxious
to finally have a personalized travel agency that I wouldn't have to
micromanage in order to receive the service I desired. Unfortunately
within ninety seconds of sitting down with the owner of the travel
agency, I knew the meeting wouldn't result in a sale for his company.

He began with these words: "Todd, I'd like to tell you a little bit about our company." And away he went. For nearly twenty minutes, he told me how the agency began, how much business it was doing, and why he felt we should use the agency. He then launched into a showering of features and benefits like the CD-ROM that I would receive every quarter to give me an ongoing listing of hotels and restaurants. He told me about the toll-free line I would be able to use as a result of our "premier" status with his firm. He told me about the emergency hot line, should I ever get stuck. He told me about the quarterly reports I would receive to help me manage the expenses of travel more appropriately. On and on he went, talking about all the things he thought I might need. And finally, he said, they would make me an unlimited supply of luggage tags.

Then came the classic line: "Todd, we'd like to ask you for your business." Isn't that what salespeople have been taught? To ask for the business?

With my arms crossed, I replied, "I'm not very motivated to give it to you." And I wasn't. I hadn't so much as opened my mouth to speak until that point.

"I could tell," he responded.

Wow, I thought, *if he could tell, I wouldn't have known it.* "For how long could you tell?" I asked him.

"About five minutes into our dialogue," he replied.

Dialogue? "That's the problem," I asserted. "We haven't had a dialogue."

He looked very confused.

I then asked him a series of questions that demonstrated what I meant: "What's my favorite airline? What's my favorite hotel? What kind of bed do I want in a hotel? Queen? King? Do I like staying on top floors or bottom floors? Near the elevator or in a corner?

Smoking or nonsmoking? Who pays for my travel—me or my clients? What times and days do I prefer to travel? And . . . how many luggage tags do I *already* own?"

The point was simple: he knew nothing about my personal values, my travel needs, or what was important to me in a relationship with a travel company. After nearly half an hour of stating his case, he knew nothing that he needed to know in order to meet my needs. The truth was that I didn't need the financial reports. I didn't need the directory or the emergency hot line. And as a frequent flyer on several airlines, I already had several luggage tags. Basically I didn't value several of the items that he launched at me as something of value.

He started the meeting talking. I started the meeting listening. And as a result, he made another fatal mistake that many salespeople make in their quest for sales. The mistake is called "arguing," and it will leave your prospects no choice but to object to your business.

STATING YOUR CASE AND SINKING YOUR CHANCES

With all the TV shows, movies, books, and news coverage about legal trials these days, it's not difficult to understand the fatal selling mistake of arguing. At the beginning of each criminal trial, each attorney takes several minutes to state the case he will be making over the course of the upcoming days or weeks or even months of the trial. This initial phase of the trial is, of course, called the "opening arguments." As you've probably seen numerous times on TV shows, movies, or the news, each attorney gets the trial officially under way by arguing for or against the claims of the person on trial—without interruption, objection, or rebuttal. And in the end, it's up to the jury to determine whose argument was more convincing. An effective, top-dollar attorney is one who knows how to present an opening argument that is both factual and compelling—an argument that not only gets the point across, but also sets the tone to sway the final decision in his favor. Although that may be an effective way to get a jury on your side, it's no way to get a prospect to buy.

In basic terms, the mistake of arguing is talking too much and listening too little. It's staking your sales success on your ability to state your case in a convincing fashion. It's mastering a monologue and then expecting the jury of your prospects to be convinced to take your side. But arguing only makes certain your sales get a death sentence. And the reason is simple: you can't build trust with a prospect if you're the only one talking. Establishing an initial level of trust takes more than flowery monologue. It takes dialogue. It takes actual conversation. There is no other way for you to know that your product or service will meet a prospect's needs.

> **Establishing an initial level of trust takes more than flowery monologue. It takes dialogue.**

Sure, you can play the presumption game: "Boy, do I have a good deal for you," or "I thought you looked like someone who might need . . ." And you can play the flattery game too: "I'm sure you're an intelligent person," or "This is something I offer to people who don't have time or money to waste. I'm sure you're one of those people." But both games are a waste of your and your prospects' time. All you really do is set yourself up for failure—and look ridiculous while doing it.

The bottom line is that it's time for salespeople to stop assuming that consumers are idiots. It's time for salespeople to start showing their prospects respect from the get-go. And a good thing to remember is that a stigma is always attached to the salesperson. Yes, unfortunately, most people still think salespeople are slick, sleazy, or underhanded. And we can no longer rely on the "a few bad apples have spoiled the bunch" excuse. You and I both know that there are more than a "few" bad apples. And your prospects know it too.

A December 2000 Gallup poll on "Honesty and Ethics in the Professions" asked those interviewed to rank thirty-two different professions based on their levels of trustworthiness.[1] The final results show that the five sales professions on the list (real estate agent, stockbroker, insurance salesperson, advertising practitioner, and car salesperson) ranked no higher than twenty-fifth, with three of the five sales professions bottoming out the list. In other words, of the eight professions ranked the least ethical and trustworthy, five were sales professions.

What that indicates is that the onus is on you to break the negative stereotype right away—every time you sell. And that starts when you throw out your opening arguments and listen immediately to your prospects—like the salesperson who walked into a meeting with a prospect who carried a huge chip on her shoulder. Without prompting, the first thing the prospect said was, "I hate salespeople—and don't give me any of that sales talk." At the time the salesperson was clutching a stack of index cards that he was planning on using for his sales pitch. But after hearing the prospect's strong words, he walked over to the trash can and tossed them. He then asked the prospect to define what she meant by *sales talk* so that he wouldn't make that mistake. Pleasantly surprised, the prospect obliged his request, and for the remainder of the meeting the two dialogued about the prospect's needs and then the salesperson's solutions. And the sale was closed that day.[2]

By taking the time to listen (and showing prospects that is your intention), you avoid monopolizing the conversation with empty sales talk. But it really shouldn't take a prospect's prompting for you to get to that place.

You must understand that you cannot chatter your way to lasting sales success, no matter *how* convincing you sound. You cannot learn a thing from your prospects by running your mouth instead of listening. You cannot determine their needs. You cannot understand their values. You cannot determine their desires. In fact, if you don't take enough time to listen, you can't even know whether your products and prospects are a good fit. In his book *The Death of 20th Century Selling,* author Dan Seidman tells a story about how he learned this lesson the hard way while serving a stint as a headhunter.

Typically a headhunter's job is to sell employees looking for work to employers looking to hire. Thus, a headhunter essentially has two prospects to please in every selling situation: the employee on a job search and the employer with a desire to hire. But only one pays the bills. Commissions are generally paid by hiring employers. When Dan was approached by the wife of a professional pitcher in the major leagues who wanted to work, he was very excited. Because she was a great salesperson, very attractive, and her husband was a well-known professional pitcher, Dan figured that selling her to a hiring company would be an easy home run. Unfortunately he got a little ahead of himself and didn't ascertain enough information from one employer before offering her skills to them.

Initially when the publisher of a magazine answered Dan's ad and agreed to pay his $12,000 fee if the magazine hired the woman, Dan thought a successful sale was in the bag. The pitcher's wife, he thought, was a shoo-in for the position. He quickly set up a meeting between the woman and the prospective employer, and he eagerly awaited the good news. He thought he had it coming when immediately following the meeting, the thrilled publisher called to tell Dan that he wanted to hire the woman and would pay his fee and her asking salary. *Grand slam*, Dan thought. But he was mistaken.

Shortly after receiving the call from the publisher, Dan received another call, this time from the woman—and she was not happy. "I can't believe you sent me there!" she screamed into the phone. The employer with whom he set up the interview was the publisher of a pornographic magazine. Dan had no idea. He was admittedly so eager to close what seemed to be an easy sale that he failed to obtain some very important information from the prospective employer first, namely, what type of magazine he published.

In retrospect, if Dan had taken more time to listen to the magazine publisher to whom he was selling, he would have known that the particular solution he was offering—the pitcher's wife—was definitely not the right fit for the magazine's needs, and it certainly wasn't appropriate for the woman.

When it comes to closing sales, *ascertaining needs is the absolute key to offering solutions that compel prospects to accept your offering*. And arguing skips this crucial step. Essentially it is presuming you know what your prospects need and then guessing that your solution will fit. But last time I checked, presumption plus guessing wasn't an equation that equaled sales success.

Sure, I'll admit that if you argue well enough, you can eventually persuade a prospect to buy from you. But that's not the way to a successful sales career. The inherent problem is that even if you do manage to argue your way to a sale, you won't have established a sound sales relationship. You'll just have convinced someone to spend money on something that may or may not meet the person's expectations. Sure, you'll have made some money, made your manager happy, or met your quota. But trust me, if you continually sell people products that disappoint or anger them, you'll not survive long in the sales business. That's because all long-term sales success is based on your ability to initiate and nurture real relationships— and sound relationships are not based on manipulation. They're based on trust.

RELATIONSHIPS TAKE MORE THAN MONOLOGUE

According to personal communications expert Dr. Theodore Zeldin, author of *Conversation: How Talk Can Change Our Lives* (Harvill Press, 1998), the way to establish trust in sales is to "create relationships in which people reciprocally reveal something of themselves, not with the purpose of selling, but with the purpose of seeing if they can each be useful to the other. I like to look at selling as a meeting of two people rather than a meeting of two commercial entities."[3] I agree wholeheartedly.

Sales relationships work no differently from everyday relationships. There are not special allowances in sales relationships that permit a seller to snub a buyer and somehow still gain his support. Establishing a successful sales relationship takes trust. And building trust takes more than presumption on your part. Just as in a healthy marriage, building and sustaining trust takes more than monologue; it takes open dialogue.

Imagine listening in on a young man and woman on a blind date—and the guy is the only one talking. He's telling her about his job that he's proud of . . . then his car that's really fast and cost a lot of money . . . and then his recent travels . . . and then his ex-girlfriend and how she just didn't understand his values . . . and then how often he goes to the gym. On and on he goes, without so much as a pause to ask the woman a question. As you listen, you're wondering whether the guy has even taken a breath during his sanctimonious fifteen-minute monologue. Finally the guy excuses himself to go the rest room.

At that point in the date, what do you think would be going through the woman's head? Would she be impressed? Would she be excited to go on another date with the guy? Would she believe him if, after dinner, he said he felt that he'd known her all his life? Would she agree with him if he said he thought the evening went really well? The truth is that the woman would probably be praying fervently that the check would come soon. She'd probably be brainstorming about how sick she needed to be in order to end the date. She might even be planning a dash for the door as soon as he slipped away to the rest room. But she most certainly wouldn't be planning their wedding. She wouldn't be compelled to hear more or to invest in a relationship with him.

And much the same happens when you make the mistake of arguing. Your prospects start thinking of excuses to end the call. They start looking for the quickest route to the door. And eventually they walk out, hang up, or slam the door in your face. My writing partner shared with me a similar arguing experience of his own. He was on the receiving end.

A salesperson for the *Los Angeles Times* called his house during the middle of the day, and as soon as Brent picked up the phone and said hello, the salesperson began his monologue. For a few minutes the man continued until Brent just couldn't take it anymore. He interrupted him and said, "Listen, man, I'm going to be honest with you—I'm allergic to newsprint, so my wife and I don't subscribe to any papers." You know what the salesperson said? "C'mon—you can't be serious?" To that, my partner said, "I'm completely serious," and he was. He *is* allergic to newsprint. But the salesperson laughed in disbelief as though Brent was lying to get off the phone. However, he wasn't laughing when my partner said good-bye and hung up. If he had taken the time to open up a little dialogue, to ask pertinent questions and listen to the answers, he would have quickly learned that what he was offering didn't meet my partner's needs. But instead he immediately began arguing his case and heard nothing but a dial tone when he was through.

CONVERSATION IS KING

Imposing a canned monologue on your prospects conveys something entirely different about your selling personality than initiating an authentic dialogue. Consider the differences between what each conveys:

DIALOGUE	MONOLOGUE
Considerate	Presumptuous
Authentic	Phony
Transparent	Underhanded
Professional	Showy
Interested in meeting needs	Interested in making money
Builds trust	Builds tension

I understand that many salespeople make the mistake of arguing without thinking about or understanding the ramifications. Maybe it's what they've been taught to do. Maybe it's what they've seen others do. Maybe it's just the only way to sell that they know. But regardless of why salespeople try to monologue their way to a sale, the results generally stay the same. And that's because people rarely buy from salespeople who won't take the time to listen to them— salespeople who convey with their mouths that making money is more important than meeting needs. And if prospects don't believe that you know them—that you genuinely want to understand their needs—you can kiss a lot of sales good-bye.

On the other hand, when you take the time to converse with your prospects, you begin to establish a foundation for a lasting sales relationship that is based on authentic needs and genuine solutions. When it comes down to it, conversation is simply the catalyst that opens the door for you to begin relating to your prospects and earning their trust.

"Real conversation," writes Dr. Zeldin, "catches fire." And he's right. *When you alter your prospecting approach from persuading to relating, you open the door to a sea of sales possibilities.* That's because people don't put trust in sales pitches—and they probably never will. They put trust in empathetic, sincere people. Remember the Gallup poll I mentioned earlier? Well, here's an interesting twist to it that demonstrates what I'm talking about. In a separate *USA Today/CNN*/Gallup poll conducted in June 2002, pollsters were asked which "groups" of people they most trusted. At #2 on the list were small business owners. So that begs the question: How is it that most people think salespeople are unethical and dishonest, but feel they can trust small-business owners—who happen to be predominantly salespeople? According to Raj Nisankarao, president of the National Business Association, "They [small business owners] have one-on-one relationships with their customers."[4] In other words, people make a clear distinction between the typical smooth-talking, silver-tongued salesperson and the business professional who takes the time to genuinely relate to them. And not just a few people make that distinction. According to the poll, 75 percent of people do.[5]

The point is simple: to build a foundation for long-term sales success, you must establish client relationships based on trust. And trust-based relationships cannot be established without genuine dialogue—without sincere conversation that opens the door for you to not only ascertain your prospects' needs but also offer solutions that truly add value to their lives.

Our company, the Duncan Group, once had an opportunity to do this, and the results speak for themselves. We were one of three sales training organizations vying for a contract with a very reputable prospect seeking ongoing training for its employees. In typical fashion, the prospect had shared with us that no decision would be made until each company had been interviewed. We looked at it as a great opportunity to set ourselves apart from the others in our arena. Furthermore, we could appreciate the prospect's desire to make a sound choice.

When Dave (the former president of our firm) and I arrived at the prospect's corporate offices, we were escorted into the top-floor conference room. As the representatives for the prospect filed into the room, you could cut the tension with a knife. Without a word, Dave and I knew that our customary prospecting approach had become all the more important. These were straight shooters, and we needed to stick to our guns. There were the head of production, the head of training, and four regional managers. And since they saw this as an interview of us, we exchanged a few pleasantries, and then the head of production said, "So, tell us about the Duncan Group."

We knew that was our moment of truth. The way we responded right then would set the tone for the meeting and eventually determine whether we would establish a new business relationship. If we had made the mistake of arguing, we would have probably responded to his opening statement by talking only about our firm. But we didn't. We turned the opportunity for a monologue into an opportunity for an open dialogue that changed the course of our meeting and subsequently the success of our relationship.

"Thanks for asking," I replied. "The Duncan Group is many things to many companies. Our overarching goal is to help our clients and their employees become more successful through our training partnerships and programs. But we can't even begin to explain how we might do that for you until we learn what's important to you about this training program."

That was the key. For forty-five minutes we dialogued. Dave and I talked to all six of them. We followed a disciplined questioning process. We listened closely to ascertain their values and needs. We learned as much as we could about how and where we could add value. And at the end of forty-five minutes of open conversation, we told them how we felt we could help them. When we asked them what they thought, they indicated that they liked how things had gone and would be in touch with us within two weeks.

On our way out of the building, Dave and I wrote six thank-you cards and dropped them in the mailbox on the first floor. The prospects would receive them the following morning. Then over the next two weeks, while we waited eagerly for their response, we sent them four client testimonials to confirm that what we told them we could do, we had actually done.

Like clockwork, a spokesperson for the prospect called exactly two weeks from our original meeting date to tell Dave that our company had been awarded the contract. Since we always ask clients why they choose us, Dave expressed thanks for the firm's trust and then posed the same question. Our new client replied, "You seemed to be the only company that knew what we were looking for." Then Dave asked what the other vendors did that the client didn't like. Our new client replied, "The others told us what they *thought* they could do for us, but none of it really seemed to fit." In short, the others had made the mistake of arguing. We, on the other hand, had taken a much different prospecting approach. And it meant a six-figure contract for our company.

OPENING AND CLOSING WITH CONVERSATION

There is power in conversation. To avoid the mistake of arguing in your sales career, you must tap into that power on a regular basis. You must adopt a new approach to selling that seeks as its primary aim to relate, not to persuade. Dr. William Isaacs, author of *Dialogue and the Art of Thinking Together* (Doubleday, 1999), says it this way: "The salesperson is not just an instrument of commerce but also an expert in human relations; and the rep's function is to make the customer feel better and understand better and feel more satisfied."[6] If the foundation of long-term sales success is trust-based relationships, the goal of selling must be to relate in a way that conveys trust, that establishes trust. And that, as Dr. Isaacs points out, is the purpose of dialogue.

But contrary to what you may think, there's more to dialogue than words being passed back and forth. "Dialogue," writes Isaacs, "is a conversation in which people think together in relationship. Thinking together implies that you no longer take your own position as final. You relax your grip on certainty and listen to the possibilities that result simply from being in a relationship with others—possibilities that might not otherwise have occurred . . .

Giving up trying to impose an agenda and genuinely listening to what is really needed and wanted in a situation is a far more potent way to operate."

> **"Giving up trying to impose an agenda and genuinely
> listening to what is really needed and wanted in
> a situation is a far more potent way to operate."**

In other words, to truly enter into a dialogue in which you begin to relate to your prospects on a level that will build trust (and subsequently close sales), you have to be willing to put your agenda aside. You have to enter into conversation with prospects for the primary purpose of learning—knowing that the only way you can be certain to meet their needs is to stop arguing your case and start relating to their cares. And there are five ways that I believe you can do this.

In order to avoid making the fatal mistake of arguing, you must regularly engage in the following five conversation practices. When these practices are prevalent in your method of selling, you'll find that your efforts establish more trust and subsequently produce more business.

1. FORGET ABOUT THE SALE.

Not for good. But you at least need to put the sale on the back burner of your mind so you can focus on really learning the needs and the values of your prospects—because sales are the by-products of effective, genuine conversation. Remember that you cannot be certain that the solution you are offering to a prospect is worth a hill of beans to him unless you've taken the time to know what the prospect is looking for.

That's why Dave and I turned our prospects' question around in the meeting I mentioned earlier. We knew that we could talk and talk and talk about our company and what we could do. But we'd just have been presuming and hoping that we knew what the prospects wanted in a sales training company, regimen, and relationship.

However, when we turned the question back on them, the tide began to change. We learned what they were looking for. And as a result, we were able to meet them right where they wanted to be met. If we had not made it a practice to "forget" the sale for those forty-five minutes, we would have been no different from the others trying to win the prospects' business. As it was, we won their trust, and that led to their business.

2. ASK, DON'T ARGUE.

Don't underestimate the importance of asking the right questions. If all you do is converse about the weather and world news, you won't learn anything about your prospects' needs. When you enter into a selling dialogue, do so with a disciplined set of questions that you've planned ahead of time. Ask questions that will help you determine whether your product or service is the right fit. Determine what your prospects are looking for, why they're looking for it, how they expect it to benefit their lives and their businesses, and when they expect to have it.

When we began a question-based dialogue with decision makers of our sales training prospect, Dave and I had two things in mind: needs and values. We knew that offering a solution that didn't take those two things into account would be futile. But because we understood the direction that the meeting needed to go in order to establish a mutually beneficial relationship, our questions were purposeful and pertinent. We recognized that what we needed to know wouldn't come unless we let them do the talking. And so we spent more time asking and listening. And they were glad to oblige this approach, and they saw our questions as a sign of genuine interest, concern, and confidence—three things that go a long way in building trust.

3. LISTEN WITH YOUR FINGERS.

Whether you're on the phone or face-to-face with prospects, taking notes is the most efficient way to ensure that the information you're gathering is sinking in. Not only that, if prospects are aware that you are taking notes, they will often see it as a sign that you are genuinely interested in what they have to say—and that you intend to use the information to help them. As we listened to the people from our sales training prospect tell us what they were looking for in an ongoing training program, Dave and I took copious notes. We listened to what they were telling us, and then we recorded what they said in an effort to solidify the information in our own minds. And when the prospects were ready to talk about solutions, we had an outline of needs to meet and values to uphold right before our eyes.

4. SEEK TO UNDERSTAND.

Verify what your prospects tell you. When Dave and I asked a question, we asked it with the purpose of ascertaining a full understanding of our prospects' answer. And many times throughout our forty-five-minute dialogue, that required us to ask second and third questions in order to come to an understanding. You must do the same. Make certain that you precisely understand your prospects' needs and values. Confirm the expectations that they've shared with you. When prospects tell you that they need something, ask them why they need it that way. I'm not suggesting you act like an inquisitive five-year-old who asks *why, why, why*, again and again, "just because." I'm telling you that your understanding of your prospects must be solid so that there is no room for presumptions. If they've answered a question and you still don't know what you need to know, ask another. If necessary, repeat what they've told you in an effort to confirm your understanding. Don't just write down answers to questions and move on. If you have any agenda in a selling situation, make it be to understand your prospects' needs and values as well as your own.

5. LISTEN AGAIN.

When appropriate and with your prospects' approval, record your meetings. Explain to your prospects up front that the purpose of recording the meeting is to give yourself an opportunity to constantly improve your efforts to meet their needs as well as the needs of your existing clients. Explain to them that it is your desire (and it should be) to never neglect or overlook what they tell you in a meeting—and although you will be taking notes and listening intently, the recording permits you to review what has been discussed in the meeting to ensure that your efforts are perfectly customized to their expectations. Not only will this practice be a gesture of your best intentions, but it will prove to be a great teaching tool.

SALES SUCCESS IS A TWO-WAY STREET

The bottom line is that selling is a shared activity that involves more than an exchange of products and money. It involves an exchange of consideration and respect, needs and values, expectations and ideas. And these things are exchanged only when you take the time to relate, to converse, and to connect.

The 2002 film titled *Door to Door* is a poignant illustration of how a salesperson's ability to connect is more important than his ability to coerce. In the film, William H. Macy plays Bill Porter, a man born with cerebral palsy who desperately wants to work for a living, despite his disability. After being turned down at numerous places of employment, Bill eventually lands a job as a door-to-door salesman with the Watkins Company because he offers to take the toughest route available. But as we learn, getting a job in the 1950s with a physical disability is not the only one of Bill's troubles. Supporting himself as a salesperson is an entirely different battle.

When Bill begins to knock on the doors of prospects along his route, his slurred speech and awkward gait scare his prospects away. Insolence becomes commonplace as doors are slammed in his face. But Bill persists with the notion that he can succeed by relating to his prospects in an authentic fashion and thus earn their respect—despite lacking "conventional" selling skills. And eventually his notion holds true.

As the story progresses, Bill's honest, relational approach wins the business of his prospects, and it wins their hearts. One by one, his prospects' tough exteriors melt away until Bill is so popular with the people along his route that he becomes a fixture in the neighborhood community. Those who once slammed the door on Bill become not only his closest customers but also his dearest friends. With his uncanny and unconventional ability to connect with people, Bill's success selling household products eventually earns him a "Salesman of the Year" award, and then another and another and another. In fact, his client base becomes so large that he has to hire an assistant to help him deliver products to his customers each day—an assistant whose heart is also won over by Bill in the process.

And there's one more detail to the story. *Door to Door* is not just a nice, feel-good script that someone fashioned in his mind. It's based on the life of its main character who is still living today. And even though he's approaching seventy years old, Bill Porter is still selling and doing it successfully. "Bill's story is so compelling," said the film's director Steven Schachter, "because he represents a kind of work ethic that's long gone—a guy who trudges through neighborhoods day after day after day, just connecting with people." That's not only a point well spoken; it's the key to overcoming the fatal mistake of arguing.

It's simple: if you desire to become a staple in your sales industry, like Bill Porter, you must learn to relate to customers from the get-go. To avoid the mistake of arguing in your sales career, you must begin your sales relationships with a connection mentality that compels you to *look to your prospects* for the key to their business. In other words, assume nothing. Make no presumptions. Like Bill Porter, just relate, listen, and relate some more. And when you can do that, you'll win your customers' business, and you'll win their hearts.

CHAPTER SEVEN

Mistake #7: Gambling

Making unplanned calls on unknown customers

My friend Brent recently shared a story from his selling days that demonstrates the gross insufficiency of another fatal mistake made by salespeople.

In 1991, Brent was hired by a privately owned financial services company to originate loans for individuals with substandard credit. His instructions were simple (or simply insufficient): pull out the phone book and start calling on local banks that offered loans only to those with good credit. The so-called prospecting strategy was aimed at taking the bad-credit loan applicants off their hands. The only problem was that Brent didn't have a single contact in the loan business. He was ambitious, however. But his enthusiastic prospecting efforts ended up being more of a wake-up call than anything else.

In preparation for his first full week on the job, Brent spent a few hours compiling a list of local banks from the phone book. He also made several anonymous phone calls to banks on his list to determine the names of the managing loan officers. That, he hoped, would at least emit a little warmth on his cold-calling attempts.

When 9:00 A.M. rolled around on what would be his first official day of prospecting, Brent was at his desk and raring to go. With his list of banks and managers' names in hand, he pulled out his trusty *Thomas Guide* and mapped the most efficient route to visit as many locations as he could in one day. He was then ready to do some serious prospecting and was confident he would return to the office later that day with at least a few solid loan leads. His day, however, would be cut short by one very disheartening reality of the prospecting gamble we call "cold calling."

Around ten o'clock that same morning, Brent hopped out of his car to pay a visit to a local bank that he knew didn't offer loans to individuals with poor credit. He had chosen this particular bank as one of his first stops because he felt confident of his chances for landing some loans there. With his best smile on, Brent walked through the door, presented himself to the receptionist, and confidently asked for the managing loan officer by name. The receptionist looked at him with a blank stare as if he'd spoken in a foreign language. After about ten seconds, she gathered her composure and asked for his name again. He told her, and she replied that the particular gentleman he was looking for was not there. Brent then asked if he could leave his card and some information for the gentleman when he returned. Again the receptionist fumbled with her words: "Um . . . how long . . . have you been working with Mr. Smith?"

"I just left him a voice mail last week," Brent replied, "and I am stopping by to discuss some potential business with him."

This time the receptionist asked my partner to wait at the front and excused herself. About two minutes later, one of the loan manager's coworkers came to the front with a very serious look on his face. He again asked Brent how he knew the man he was there to call on. In a more apprehensive voice, my partner told him. The coworker subtly dropped his head. "I'm sorry to have to tell you this," he replied solemnly, "but Mr. Smith passed away on Saturday of a heart attack."

THE ODDS ARE AGAINST YOU

For Brent, that experience was a harsh introduction to another potentially fatal mistake that salespeople make in their quest to succeed. The mistake is called "gambling," and it's essentially writing your own ticket to selling doom.

As the name suggests, gambling in your sales career is no different from placing a bet and rolling a pair of dice. In either case, your success is based on random chance, on what compulsive gamblers call "Lady Luck." And if you know anything about the gambling addiction, Lady Luck is a ruthless, unpredictable woman. Just when you think she's on your side, she'll take you for all you're worth. And something very similar happens when you rely on luck in the sales profession.

The mistake of gambling begins with a careless, even reckless, prospecting technique. It's an impulsive strategy of calling on anybody at any time, assuming that the more people you call, the greater your chances for landing a sale. It's betting on the law of averages, which in gambling means that the greater number of bets you place, the greater your probability for success. But the truth is that even in casino gambling, the odds for success are never high, regardless of how many bets you place. And the house always has the edge.

At the roulette table your odds for winning on one spin of the wheel are only 2.6 percent, or 1 in 38. Over the long haul, mathematical probability indicates that if you bet a modest $100 an hour on roulette, you will lose an average of $5.26. Most people, however, lose much more. In the dice-rolling game of craps, your odds for winning with one roll of the dice vary from a mere 16.7 percent to a minuscule 2.8 percent, depending on your bet. In the card game of blackjack, you have only a 5 percent chance of being dealt a 21-value hand. Gambling—whether in a casino or in a sales career—is just a game of probabilities in which you never have the upper hand.

But contrary to the law of averages, increasing your number of "bets" (or cold calls) in sales doesn't necessarily increase your odds for success—it just seems that way. The truth is that when you factor in the increasing amount of time and money you must spend to keep betting (or prospecting) in order to land a sale, your true odds for being successful usually stay about the same, no matter how long you gamble. In other words, landing 1 sale after 50 calls in 2 days ends up being no different from landing 5 sales after 250 calls over the course of 4 days. Sure, the second scenario produces 4 more sales than the first, but it's still only a 2 percent success rate. Or—if you remove your rose-colored visor and look at it the way you should—a 98 percent failure rate.

The mistake of gambling is the "surely I'm due" approach to selling—the "if I make enough calls, I will eventually succeed" approach to prospecting. And if you rely on it long enough, like a compulsive gambler, you'll eventually end up broke.

Gambling is essentially trying to build your career on a foundation of chance cold calling. It's hedging your success on the ridiculous idea that people *like* being interrupted to discuss a product or service for which they may not have a need. Think about the times you've been cold-called. No matter what time of day it is, do you like it? I doubt it. No one really does. It's bothersome. It's insensitive. It's presumptuous. And whether it's made during the day or at night, it produces resistance and kills your momentum. So why in the world would any salesperson put stock in such a strategy? Because we're impatient? Because we're disillusioned? Because we're stubborn and simply refuse to face the facts? Whatever the reason, the odds for succeeding in sales with a cold-calling strategy are never good. Most incentive-based sales managers use the following statistics to incite their salespeople to hit the ground running, or in this case, cold calling.

- One sale needs six qualified presentations (phone calls, face-to-face meetings, and so forth).

- For six presentations you need twenty-four prospects.

- To have twenty-four prospects, you need one hundred suspects.

In other words, to make one sale via cold calling, the accepted norm is that you must expect to weed through at least one hundred potential prospects and make no less than twenty-four calls to those you deem qualified prospects. Do those odds sound good to you? At a 4.2 percent probability of success, those odds are only slightly better than winning on your first spin at the roulette table and slightly worse than being dealt a hand of 21 in blackjack.[1] And if you think those odds are disheartening, consider how the odds are only getting worse.

Sales frauds are everywhere these days, and the government and consumers are beginning to raise their defenses. The Fraud Information Center, a branch of the National Consumers League, reports that from the beginning of 2000 to the end of 2002, consumers in the U.S. lost more than $10 million of their hard-earned money to sales scams.[2] That comes out to an average loss of $1,160 per sales fraud victim per year. And do you know how the majority of the fraudulent salespeople went about their business? Of the six most common methods of initial contact that the fraudulent salespeople used . . .

1. Phone

2. Mail

3. Print

4. Fax

5. TV/radio

6. In person

. . . the highest percentage (45 percent) used the telephone to spread their seedy scam. In other words, there are more than innocent, well-meaning salespeople using the phone to make their cold calls. *If cold calling was simply an insufficient battle strategy in the past, it's truly a shot in the dark now.*

FACING THE FACTS

The vast majority of consumers don't like sales gamblers—they insult their intelligence and waste their time. Maybe that's why consumers are increasingly screening calls. In the article "Can Telemarketing Save Itself?" marketing expert Joanna Krotz reported that an American Teleservices Association survey in 2002 found that "roughly four out of 10 Americans (39%) subscribe to a caller ID service. For younger consumers, aged 25–34, that percentage jumped to more than half (54%)."[3] What that means is that most people enjoy getting an unexpected earful about as much as they enjoy getting an earache. They're both painfully inconvenient and something they wish they didn't have to deal with.

As I write this, the National Do Not Call Registry is going into effect, which will eventually make it impossible for phone-dependent salespeople to rely on a gambling-type strategy to succeed. And don't think you're off the hook if you don't use the phone to sell your wares. A face-to-face gambling strategy is equally ineffective and even more awkward than cold calling on the phone. Put it this way: whether you gamble in person, via snail mail, via e-mail, or via the phone, it's an insufficient strategy that is annoying to most victims on the receiving end and embarrassing to you.

> Whether you gamble in person, via snail mail, via e-mail, or via the phone, it's an insufficient strategy that is annoying to most victims on the receiving end and embarrassing to you.

It was actor/comedian Jerry Seinfeld who best conveyed the attitude of consumers today with regard to cold-calling salespeople who use the phone to peddle their products. On an episode of his legendary sitcom, he answered a phone call during dinner, and by his tone you knew it was a salesperson making a cold call. He attempted in vain to get off the phone, and when he realized the salesperson wasn't going to relent, Seinfeld asked the man if he could call him back. When the salesperson agreed, Seinfeld asked for his home phone number. Then when the salesperson asked why he wanted his home phone number, the actor retorted that he intended to call the salesperson back at *his* house and interrupt *his* dinner to discuss whatever he was calling about.

Despite the fact that many sales companies still insist that gambling is just the nature of prospecting, nothing could be further from the truth. Gambling is an uphill, in-the-snow, walking-backward-for-two-miles kind of battle. It's placing a big, sleazy-salesperson stigma on your forehead that people can see (or hear in your voice) for miles. And given the lofty number of sales frauds every year and the popularity of the Do Not Call Registry, you are lucky to ever get over that hurdle. But even if you end up making a sale from a gambling strategy, it's still unlikely that you've built trust. Most cold-calling strategies are based on either high pressure or subtle deceit. And neither is any way to start a sales relationship. Both create a measure of tension between you and your prospect, and as you certainly know from your personal relationships, tension doesn't help create trust. It usually does just the opposite.

The following graph illustrates how tension in a sales call (on the phone or in person) acts as the antagonist of trust:

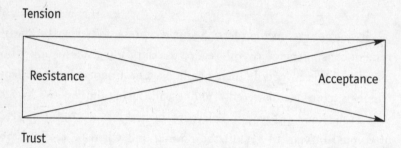

As you can see from the graph, trust and tension are at opposite ends of the selling spectrum. Tension creates resistance. Trust leads to acceptance. And routinely, when one is increasing, the other tends to decrease. In other words, when tension is at its highest, trust is at its lowest, and so is the probability of a prospect's acceptance of your offer.

On the other hand, as tension decreases, so does resistance, thus increasing a prospect's trust and the probability that she will accept your offer. Therefore, it is in your best selling interest to travel the path of least resistance, so to speak—to go down the path where tension is continually reduced and trust is continually advanced.

And gambling is certainly not this path. Gambling is trying to succeed by selling along the path where tension and resistance remain high. And you will never achieve consistent success that way. I learned this early in my career.

REDUCING PROSPECTING TENSION

When I began my selling career in my early twenties, I felt I had a strong ability to put a positive spin on any situation. One of my first days in the field made me seriously question my abilities, however.

I was given a territory that stretched thirty miles, and within that territory, there were at least twenty-five key accounts with whom I was to develop a business relationship. In each one of these offices, there were between forty and one hundred prospects who would have a use for my product, and if I did it right, they might use my product as many as three to five times a month. I was in the real estate loan business, and these prospects were real estate agents. I figured it was quite an opportunity for me to succeed.

On my first morning, I traveled about twenty miles south of my office to make my first cold call. I was excited. I had some information that I was going to drop off. I had some nice brochures that outlined some of my company's key products and the costs for each of them. But when I pulled into the first office's parking lot, something gripped me—and hard. *On whom was I going to call? How was I going to call on them? What if they didn't want to be called on?*

My fears elevated as I walked through the front door of the office and stared into a sea of faces. Then I watched as potential prospects immediately became "busy." They picked up their phones

131

and talked to no one. They engaged in conversations with their peers so they could avoid having one with me. They did whatever they could to dodge an encounter with another salesperson. So I talked with the receptionist, and after a few mindless minutes of shallow conversation, she told me where to leave my information. And that was it. No contact, no prospects, and consequently no business.

I regrouped and went to my next account. Same results. Then to my next account. Same results. After five attempts, I could no longer put a positive spin on making cold calls. I was getting rejected. My self-esteem was waning. And the only sensible thing to do was to stop making cold calls. But, I wondered, how would I explain this to my boss? "Todd, how was your first day?" he would ask. "Well, Bob, not real good. After five cold calls and a ton of rejection, I decided that it would be stupid to call on the other twenty accounts . . . so I went to the beach."

While my decision didn't demonstrate the best work ethic, quitting that day was one of the smartest things I ever did as a salesperson. Essentially I recognized that calling on people who were not aware I was going to call on them was the fast track to rejection, depression, and declining productivity.

After some thinking time at the beach, I called a friend in the real estate business and asked if I could come by and simply watch how my peers were calling on *his* office. He said okay. For three hours, I observed twenty salespeople come through the front door of that office—and not one of them had an appointment. They did the exact same thing I had done earlier in the day—and were met with the same results.

Then around 4:00 P.M. a pleasant man with a nice leather portfolio under his arm walked through the front door. He wore a genuine smile as he approached the receptionist and said, "My name is John, and I have an appointment with Paula." *Finally, someone different,* I thought. It wasn't long before Paula was there to greet him, and the two of them disappeared into her office. I had to wait and see the outcome. When they emerged forty-five minutes later, John said to Paula, "Thanks for your time. I look forward to a long and profitable business partnership." I felt some excitement return to me. Never again would I sell like the twenty cold callers who walked through the door earlier. I would figure out what John did, and I would sell like him.

Shortly thereafter, I connected with John. He was highly successful in my industry and was open to sharing with me the secret of his prospecting success. He shared three "rules" with me that changed the course of my professional sales career for good:

1. Never make a call on prospects who don't know you're going to call on them.

2. When you make the call, make sure they're excited to have you call on them.

3. Never leave a call without adding more value than you have received.

These three rules are more than an inspiration to sell. They are ultimately the foundation for you to avoid the mistake of gambling in your sales career—just as they were for me.

Prospecting success doesn't depend upon how many calls you make. If that were the case, compulsive sales gambling might be a decent strategy. The truth is that *prospecting success ultimately depends upon how many calls make you sales.*

PRODUCTIVITY MEANS SALES NUMBERS

The false notion that many sales managers leave with their salespeople is that greater numbers mean greater productivity. That's why so many salespeople are held accountable for the amount of time they are on the phone and the amount of calls they make. Even in my first job I was asked to place twenty-five blind "bets" in one day. I wasn't taught how to get in touch with all those potential prospects in a way that would usher in their trust and acceptance. I was just told to go for it. But now I know that if I had kept going for it, all I would have gotten was broke. Fortunately I saw a glitch in the so-called strategy and did something about it. You may not have been as fortunate.

You may be reading this chapter and slapping your forehead in disgust and frustration at all the time you have wasted in your sales career on the mistake of gambling. But the past is now the past—even if you made a gambling mistake yesterday. Today's truth is that you can still do something about the future of your sales career if you're willing to change your prospecting strategy and do away with gambling for good. Contrary to what you were taught to assume, greater numbers don't mean greater productivity. It's actually the other way around. *Greater productivity in prospecting means a greater number of sales.*

After attending my company's High Trust Sales Academy, one sales professional did away with cold calling altogether and adopted a prospecting strategy based on the three rules I learned when I was a new salesperson. He was interested in closing lots of sales, but not in making lots of calls (and I imagine you're in the same boat). Within eight short weeks of applying a nongambling strategy, he had already met with thirty-seven new prospects and received business from thirty-three of them. If you don't think a highly productive prospecting strategy is vital to your career longevity, he would beg to differ.

Of course, prospecting matters. It's the first active step you must take as a salesperson. And if you gamble with your first step, there's no guarantee that you will have an opportunity to take another. The only thing gambling guarantees is that you will have to prospect longer and harder to be successful. Gambling is unproductive. You must accept that truth. But when you begin to implement a prospecting strategy in which productivity is always high and the stakes for success remain in your favor, you will begin to see that gambling is a game that should remain in casinos, not in sales careers.

THE FUNDAMENTALS OF PROSPECTING PRODUCTIVITY

There are four fundamental prospecting strategies that you must implement in order to replace a gambling game plan in your sales career. Essentially each strategy builds on the three rules that my friend John introduced me to when I was a budding salesperson. So that they are fresh in your mind, here are the three rules again in summary:

1. Never call on a prospect who isn't expecting your call.

2. Never call on a prospect who isn't excited to talk to you.

3. Never end a prospecting call without adding more value than you have received.

Basically each of the four strategies I will share with you warms up your initial prospecting calls and increases your prospects' propensity for trusting you. This increases the probability that prospects will accept your offer. However, before I continue, it's important to keep in mind that the primary action for removing gambling from your sales career is simply putting an end to cold calling. It's a waste of your selling hours, it's highly unproductive, and it's putting your sales future in the hands of mere chance. I realize that for some, putting an end to cold calling is much easier said than done. But as I explain the following prospecting strategies to you, I'm confident that you will begin to see how it is very possible to grow a successful sales business without relying on a single roll of the dice.

1. CONSISTENTLY SEW A COMMON THREAD.

There are a number of innovative and effective ways in which you can warm up prospects before ever approaching them in the first place, but by far the best method is via a referral call from someone whom both you and the prospect know and respect. By having a mutual friend or acquaintance contact a prospect on your behalf and getting an okay for you to contact that individual, you move your prospecting efforts out of the unnerving category of cold calling. In addition, you gain a measure of credibility with the prospect before making contact. As a result of my introduction, my brother Jeff, who is a top financial planner, just landed an account with the person from whom I buy my Mercedes. And now he's being referred to all the other salespeople in the dealership—without having to make a single cold call.

Your referral source could be a strategic partner, a noncompetitive colleague who has worked with the prospect before, a family member, or a mutual friend. The point is not what role your referral source usually plays; the important point is that he or she is someone whom your prospect trusts and respects. When that is the case, calling on a prospect is simply meeting a friend of a friend.

2. REGULARLY STRETCH CLIENT SATISFACTION.

If you have certain clients with whom you have a great rapport and a solid history of business together, make your clients' satisfaction go further than just their repeat business. When you and a client have a solid relationship built on trust, utilize that person to help you build rapport with new prospects. Obviously clients may refer prospects to you without your asking, but never assume that will happen. As you continually foster your current client relationships to higher levels of trust, if it's appropriate and legal in your industry, give your clients great incentives to refer their friends, families, and colleagues to you. Seek to add more and more value to them so that when you ask for added value from them in the form of referrals, they won't think twice. Their natural reaction will be to help you in any way that they can.

I'm not telling you anything that's revolutionary. I'm simply telling you that in order for clients to be excited about helping you prospect, you need to make it worth their while. In short, for you to ask them to help, you need to make a sacrifice too. Sure, good business will generally breed word-of-mouth referrals. But when you offer creative, valuable incentives to your clients to incite them to work for you, they tend to do more than just think of your name when your product or service comes up in conversation. They literally begin to hit the pavement for you.

My friend Mike told me about a couple of his innovative friends who own a successful financial services company. To help get their company off the ground, they regularly offered a healthy portion of their commission to fellow agents who referred clients to them. And now, just two years later, they no longer make cold calls. In fact, the vast majority of their business is based on unsolicited referrals. And that keeps their pipeline continually full.

3. GET OUT MORE.

Focus on building relationships outside of work. If you really did your homework, you'd be pleasantly surprised at how many people in your realm of influence know people interested in your product. The problem is that so many salespeople get caught up in a "work relationships are for work, and nonwork relationships are for pleasure" mentality. As a result they never think outside the realm of their work environment when prospecting. But the truth is that all preselling activity should begin with the question: "Whom do I know who knows whom I want to know?" That's the best place to begin prospecting because it ensures that you will have a common thread with whomever comes from that pool—something we discussed in the first strategy.

Get out more, and take the initiative to get to know more people about whom you can ask the above question. Get more involved in your local church. Become a member of a local club or organization that promotes something you are genuinely interested in. Befriend the people you see on a regular basis while grocery shopping or getting gas or buying clothes. The more people you get to know, the bigger your pool of potential prospects becomes.

Please understand that I am not suggesting that you just get to know people to use them. Nobody likes it when a person he has just met hits him up for a business lead. I'm just proposing that you expand the horizons of your friendships—that you understand that prospecting really doesn't need to be a stuffy, businesslike activity. In fact, if you are a genuine friend to many people, prospecting can be nothing more than friendly conversation.

4. TAKE YOUR FOCUS OFF SELLING.

I'm not kidding. Prospecting is less about your ability to sell than it is about your ability to build trust and foster new relationships. Too many salespeople make the mistake of entering into a prospecting call with such a business mentality that they come off square and unapproachable. But prospects don't respond well to people who sound as if they're selling something. They respond to people who are courteous and genuine—people who are just regular people—people they could see themselves befriending. That's the kind of connection you need to make in order to begin building a lasting sales relationship. And it doesn't come as a result of how you sell. That kind of connection comes as a result of how you relate. And when your prospecting actions are representing not only yourself but also a family member, friend, or colleague, making that type of impression is of greater interest to you.

There are certainly more ways that you can steer your prospecting efforts away from a gambling tendency, but the four we have just discussed are necessary strategies that you cannot brush off—especially if you expect to maintain a high probability of success. You've probably heard it said that the most successful salespeople "make their own luck." That, of course, is just a play on words. It is not an endorsement of sales gambling. What it essentially means is that the salespeople who are met with the most success tend to be the ones who consistently do the right things—the salespeople who are not just ambitious, but ambitious in the right direction. Their selling "cards" come up aces much more often, not because they are lucky, but because they are strategic and consistent. They know where to find prospecting aces—and they continually play from that same deck. And after all that's been said, if you still insist on luck being a part of your prospecting strategy, that's the only kind of luck that should remain—the kind that you *make* through strategic, productive prospecting.

CHAPTER EIGHT

Mistake #8: Begging

*Seeking your customers' business before
earning your customers' trust*

Before heading down to a local Toyota dealership, Sheryl and I had spent some time determining which models we were interested in. Our boys are growing up fast, and with their skateboards, snowboards, surfboards, motorcycles, and baseball equipment, we simply needed more space. After much research and discussion, we settled on a Toyota Sequoia.

About a mile from our house was a Toyota dealership. Convenient, we thought. That would be where we would begin our journey. But upon our arrival, I knew we were in for trouble as a salesperson approached us. It was clearly his turn to spin the sales wheel of fortune and try to land a sale. As he left his strategic perch facing the customer parking lot and glided like a hawk toward us, I said to myself, *Here we go again.* And he didn't let me down.

He started with some shallow, meaningless engagement—not bothering to introduce himself or ask our names. And while I tried to give him the cold shoulder, he persisted with his agenda. Eventually I responded by telling him that we were looking for a Toyota Sequoia and wanted to test-drive one.

His unfeeling response surprised me: "We don't have any. The car is very popular and they fly off the lot the minute they get here."

I didn't know whether he was telling the truth or just setting me up, so I asked if there were any in the service department that we could maybe look at or just sit in to see how we liked the feel.

Again his answer was curt. "We're not allowed to do that," he asserted.

I was beginning to wonder how the guy ever made a sale. Sheryl and I had come to the dealership to buy—we didn't really need to be talked into it. In essence, we were not a hard sell. We had expected the salesperson to be willing to help us, to show us that he was genuinely interested in our business, and at least to make an attempt to build rapport with us. But apparently that was too much to ask.

"If I could locate one for you at another dealership," he continued in a presumptuous fashion, "would you buy it now?"

Was he kidding? It was then crystal clear to me—he was more interested in getting the sale than he was in earning it. He expected us to pay his keep when he wasn't willing to earn it in the first place. He was looking for a handout and we weren't giving him one.

Firmly I told him no, we wouldn't buy it.

In response he asked for our name and phone number so he could call us when a Sequoia came in. *Why not?* I thought. *Maybe he's just having a bad day after all.* So I gave him our information.

He never called. I can't say I expected an outcome that was any different. At least he was consistent . . . consistent in making another fatal mistake, typical of too many salespeople, called "begging."

BEGGARS CAN'T BE CHOOSERS

I'm sure most of us first heard the expression from our parents when we were still kids. You had probably asked and asked and asked for something, such as a new pair of jeans or some new shoes for school, and when you received the item, you weren't completely satisfied. Maybe the shoes weren't real Nikes or the jeans weren't real Guess, and you wanted the best. You expected to receive one thing and ended up receiving another. And even though you hadn't bought the item with your hard-earned money, you found reason to complain a little. Maybe you even shed a selfish tear or two.

And then, like clockwork, came the age-old response: "Beggars can't be choosers, son . . . Honey, I'm sorry, beggars can't always be choosers." And if you were like most kids, you probably didn't have a clue what the expression meant—other than indicating you weren't going to get what you wanted.

Well, apparently many salespeople never grow up. By the actions of sales professionals like the Toyota salesperson I mentioned, many forget to ask what that expression meant when they get older. Either that is the case, or many salespeople are still ignoring their parents' wisdom. But whatever the excuse, the bottom line is basically still the same: beggars really *can't* be choosers. And to ignore that wisdom doesn't make things any better—especially in the world of sales.

Essentially the fatal mistake of begging is trying to close sales without earning your customers' trust. It's looking for handouts. It's asking for prospects' business without an ounce of indication that they are ready to buy from you. It's petitioning for a sale without earning your prospect's vote and then, like a spoiled six-year-old, complaining that you didn't get what you wanted when your prospect says no. And if that becomes your way of doing business, you'll end up begging for more than sales. You'll end up begging your boss for your job.

To consistently make the mistake of begging in your sales career is to assume with your actions that people always have one hand on their wallet and another on their pen. It's presuming that people are always ready to buy and willing to sign the paperwork . . . if only you ask. But that's not the way it works, is it? People are usually not lined up out the door to give you their business. You're a consumer; you know how it goes. Even if you're in the market for a particular product or service, there's no guarantee that you'll buy from the first salesperson to show up—especially if he does nothing to show you that he values your business.

> **People are usually not lined up out the door to give you their business. You're a consumer; you know how it goes.**

Now, I realize that there are times when consumers simply want something badly enough that they just slap money into the hand of the first salesperson they see—and that is the consumers' prerogative. But handouts are a rare exception in the world of sales, and you certainly cannot rely on them if you're interested in remaining a salesperson for long.

As I'm sure you know, even when your particular market is hot or your product is flying off the proverbial shelves, you still have to earn your keep. There is still competition. Customers still have the final say. And most people don't hand their money to just anybody. People generally need a good reason to give you their business—and "just because I asked" is not good enough. One salesperson learned this in a rather awkward fashion.

While sitting in the office of the owner of a very large company, he began to ask for business with nothing more than small talk to set up his so-called close. He had sold to the company in the past, but the business transactions were few and far between. He'd never really followed up with the company, and subsequently he'd never given the company reason to give him more business. And in the middle of the salesperson's begging episode, the owner gave a not-so-subtle clue to what he thought of the salesperson's tactics. Getting up from his desk, the owner proceeded to walk to the bathroom adjacent to his office. Then leaving the door open, he called to the salesperson to continue talking.

The salesperson was sidetracked, but persisted to beg. "You have to give me an order," he pleaded, "or the other salespeople in the office will think I'm a bad salesperson."

To that, the owner aptly responded, "How about I just give you a signed letter saying that I think you are a very good salesperson?" And thus the fate of the sales professional was sealed. He left the owner's office without an order, but undoubtedly with a lingering impression.[1]

The primary problem with begging is that it's an upside-down approach to selling. It's putting your selling emphasis on asking for business when it should be on building rapport—on receiving buy-in. In short, *begging is an impatient approach to selling that puts the onus of success on your ability to close rather than connect.*

Take a look at the two diagrams that illustrate the difference between begging your way to a sale and establishing buy-in first, then asking for business when trust has already been established.

DIAGRAM 1: BEGGING FOR BUSINESS

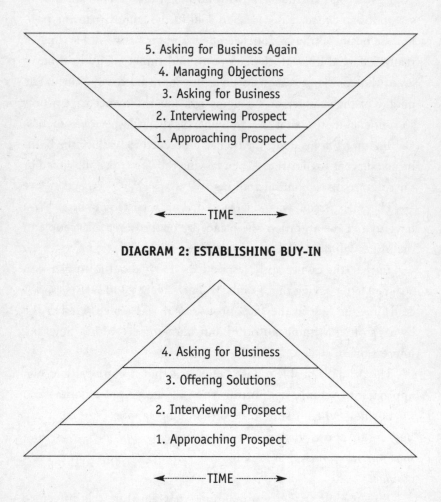

DIAGRAM 2: ESTABLISHING BUY-IN

As you can see from Diagram 1, when salespeople make the fatal mistake of begging, they spend very little time on the initial trust-building steps of the selling process, namely, approaching and interviewing their prospects. They typically get prospects on the phone or walk into prospects' offices and spend a few minutes inducing some meaningless small talk that doesn't ascertain a single need related to the product or service they'd like to sell. Consequently they don't spend any time truly offering solutions (the third step in Diagram 2) because they don't take the time to determine their prospects' needs. And in the end, they spend the majority of their time asking for business . . . or if we're honest, *begging* for business again and again because they never received their prospects' buy-in in the first place. But that's an upside-down approach to closing a sale, and eventually it will turn your career upside down and empty your pockets.

To be successful in the sales profession, you must understand that connecting with your customers is everything. The truth is, when you take the time to earn a prospect's trust at the outset, asking for business is just a formality. And there is certainly no begging necessary. Consequently, as Diagram 2 shows, asking for business takes up the least amount of your selling time. When you've spent enough time connecting with a customer during the first two steps of the selling process (approaching and interviewing your prospects) and have received buy-in there, your sales tend to close themselves.

FIVE WAYS TO RECEIVE BUY-IN . . . AND BUSINESS

Remember our nightmare salesperson at the Toyota dealership? Well, the next salesperson Sheryl and I experienced that day was quite a contrast, for all the right reasons. About an hour away from our home was a second Toyota dealership. Upon our arrival, we felt no pressure to deal with a begging salesperson. In fact, we took our time surveying the lot, and when we were ready, we met up with an unassuming, friendly salesperson named Bill. After a casual introduction, we told Bill that we were interested in purchasing a Sequoia.

"That's a great car," he responded. "It's receiving a lot of praise from the industry."

We nodded in agreement. Then in an effort to begin ascertaining our needs, he asked, "Are you familiar with the different versions and options for that car?"

We told him that we weren't. So for the next thirty minutes, at our request, we sat down with Bill as he asked us a series of questions to help determine precisely what we were looking for. Then once we had established the exact car we wanted to purchase, he asked if we'd like him to check the dealership's inventory. We said yes, and within five minutes Bill was telling us that although they did not have the precise car in stock that would meet our needs, they could have one at the dealership within three weeks. He went on to say that if we were interested, he'd be glad to order the car and reserve it for us, with no obligation to purchase it when it came in. We said yes and told him that in the meantime we would try to test-drive an SUV at a dealership closer to our home so that we'd be able to make an educated decision in three weeks. Bill told us that it was his pleasure to help us and that he would be in touch soon to let us know the status of our order.

Over the next three weeks, Bill contacted us on a regular basis. He gave us weekly updates on the status of the car's delivery. Twice he called to make sure there were no options we had changed our minds about. And then three days before schedule, Bill called to let us know the car had arrived. At that time, we told him that we'd made the decision to purchase the car from him and would like to pick it up as soon as we could. No finagling. No hassling. No begging. Then, as if Bill hadn't already done enough to earn our business, he went the extra mile and arranged train tickets for Sheryl and me from San Diego to the train station closest to the dealership, where he would personally pick us up. And when we arrived on the train a few days later, we were not only excited to pick up our new car but also glad to give our business to a salesperson who had truly earned it the right way.

To understand how Bill earned our sale without a scrap of begging, here are five ways to ensure that your prospects buy into you before you ask them for their business. When you adhere to these five, you will find that you have to do very little "selling" in order to close sales.

1. SAY SOMETHING NEW.

Never let it be said of you, "I've heard it all before." If you can't market and/or offer your product in a fresh and innovative way, don't offer it at all. There is far too much competition for you to be selling run-of-the-mill products in a run-of-the-mill fashion, regardless of your industry. Set yourself apart. Determine unique ways to appeal to your customers and meet their needs, even if that simply means being completely authentic, like Bill, in a notoriously dubious industry. Make it your goal not to be like the rest.

2. BE THE FIRST TO ADD VALUE.

Don't ever expect something from a prospect unless you have already added value. And by the way, having the privilege of meeting you is not a perceived value to your prospects. Do something up front to let your prospects know that it is your primary goal to add real value to their lives through not only your product, but also your service. Bill made this very clear to Sheryl and me from the outset. He allowed us some breathing room and did not shove his agenda down our throats, as the other salesperson had done. Next he sought to ascertain our needs before so much as a peep about the sale. And then he asked whether we wanted to move forward at each step of the way. Bill's ability to add value up front without mentioning the sale was one of the biggest factors that compelled us to buy from him despite having to wait three weeks for our product.

> Do something up front to let your prospects know that it is
> your primary goal to add real value to their lives through
> not only your product, but also your service.

3. BE THE FIRST TO SAY THANK YOU.

Bill left no doubt in our minds that he considered it a privilege to meet us and have the opportunity to meet our needs. Without assuming we were ready to buy his product, he made it evident that even if we chose to "think about it" in the end or even not buy the car, he would treat us with the same level of appreciation and respect. You must do the same with your prospects. Always appreciate the *opportunity* to meet your prospects' needs, not just their "yes" to doing business.

4. RESPECT YOUR PROSPECTS' TIME.

Not once did Bill presume that our time was his to waste. Not once did he burst into a feature-dropping rant. Not once did he move forward with any step in the transaction without first asking us if that was what we wanted. Bill demonstrated a genuine respect for our time, and as a result, we had no problem spending more than an hour with him. We felt that he was always aware of our time. We trusted Bill because we saw that he valued our time as much as we did. And in order to gain rapport with your prospects, you must do the same. Don't ever presume that your prospects want to hear *anything* from you. Offer first. Or let them ask. But don't blurt or babble. Furthermore, never take a single step toward closing a deal until you have first asked your prospects' permission to move forward. And by the way, don't ask until you have already done the first three things on this list. If you ask your prospects whether they want to move forward without giving them a reason to want to move forward, you'll be seen as presumptuous and over-aggressive.

5. DON'T STOP ONCE THE SALE SEEMS IMMINENT.

If during a selling transaction, you've done the previous four things on the list and it seems that a sale is going to close, don't become overeager and forget yourself. Bill never did assume that we would buy. At least he didn't show it. Inside he may have had a good feeling that the transaction was going well, but that never caused him to let up on setting himself apart, adding value, being appreciative, or respecting our time. Those things were just part of how he did business, regardless of whether we bought. And even after we bought, he still did them—and still does to this day. That characteristic is vital to your efforts in building trust.

It's one thing to do everything right in order to get the prospect interested, but it's another to remain consistent when you know the prospect is about to sign on the dotted line. If your stripes change then, you'll taint an otherwise strong rapport. And even if you do still close the sale, your new clients probably won't remain with you for

THE TOP TEN MISTAKES SALESPEOPLE MAKE & HOW TO AVOID THEM

long. That's because earning trust from your prospects is an ongoing activity that requires, at the very least, consistency of character.

The main reason your actions must lead to buy-in first is that if prospects don't trust you, they will remain reluctant to buy from you, no matter how many times you ask for their business. It's simple: buy-in must come first or you *will* have to beg to close a sale. And handouts are no way to earn a living—especially when you don't have to. The key to closing sales without begging is to ask for business only when you have . . .

- set yourself apart from other salespeople in your industry

- added value up front

- demonstrated your appreciation for the opportunity to earn their business

- ascertained their needs and values while respecting their time

- confirmed that they would like to proceed each step of the way

When your authentic actions create an environment that breeds buy-in with your prospects, closing sales tends to become an afterthought. That doesn't mean you won't still have to ask for a prospect's business. It just means that asking won't be a chore—it won't be begging. It will be the natural conclusion to your prospect interactions and the natural beginning to your client relationships. If you follow the five principles well, as Bill did, you will probably find that prospects are willing to wait for your product, even when they can get it sooner elsewhere. And in the end, you and I would probably rather buy from people like Bill than anyone else because they treat us like fellow human beings—not, as begging would suggest, like a piece of meat. Breaking a cycle of begging in your sales career is really just a matter of putting yourself in your prospects' shoes and doing to them what you'd want done to you in the same scenario.

TRADING PLACES

In the now legendary 1983 film *Trading Places*, two greedy Philadelphia commodity brokers, Randolph and Mortimer Duke (Ralph Bellamy and Don Ameche), bet the sum of $1 on what they call a "scientific experiment," namely, that they can remove Louis (Dan Aykroyd), the somewhat naive pawn who is heading their company, and successfully replace him with a common but charismatic homeless man named Valentine (Eddie Murphy). The bet is a hideously self-righteous one: Can the two micromanaging brothers play puppet master and take any-old-body—even a homeless man with no business experience—and make him play the part of their successful protégé?

If you've seen the film, you know that the experiment backfires, not because it doesn't work, but because it does. When the homeless Valentine is initially transplanted into the shoes of the well-to-do Louis, he lives it up. He celebrates his good fortune by moving into Louis's corporate-owned house, driving his expensive car, and spending his money. But the longer Valentine remains in Louis's shoes, the more he begins to see things from his perspective. And the longer Louis remains out of luck and on the street, the more he wakes up to the reality of why his former bosses would fire him and replace him with someone like Valentine. In short, the two men begin to see both ends of the spectrum. And with a shared perspective and a common goal, Valentine and Louis take down the conceited, crooked brothers in grand style.

While the film does poke fun at many superficial aspects of American society in the early 1980s, it also gives rise to a very earnest concept: the idea that a person in one environment can best learn the perspective of a person in another environment by literally putting himself in the other's place or, as the film's title suggests, by trading places with the other person. And that's precisely the concept you need to adopt in order to do away with trying to beg your way to selling success.

The fact is that if more salespeople spent more time in their customers' shoes, they'd more readily and accurately learn the perspective they need in order to be highly successful at their jobs. Furthermore, they'd more quickly adopt a natural discipline of following the five principles we discussed earlier. And if you think about it, that shouldn't be very difficult. Aren't all salespeople customers as well?

Aren't you learning something as a consumer that you can apply as a salesperson? Of course you are. We're treated unfairly at times, and so we know how *not* to treat our customers. Just as I experienced with the first Toyota salesperson, we're rubbed the wrong way at times, and so we know how *not* to rub our customers the wrong way. And sometimes, as with my experience with Bill, we're treated just right. Therefore, we should know how to give our customers the same level of service. But some who end up begging don't seem to understand that all around them is a sea of lessons and opportunities to improve.

To be empathetic is to demonstrate a shared perspective. And when it comes down to it, there is absolutely no reason why every salesperson cannot adopt a selling strategy that takes into account how his customers want to feel—because, to put it plainly, they know how they want to feel as a customer. Of course, not every customer is the same. Each has different views, values, and expectations. But when it comes to how people like to be treated, there's not much differentiation.

As we discussed earlier, people like Bill sell well because they treat their customers like real people instead of a piece of meat. Salespeople like Bill are successful because they put themselves in their customers' shoes and treat them as they'd want to be treated in the same situation. And you know what? If you're not sure what it means to treat people with value, respect, honor, and honesty, then ask your customers what it means to them. I'm serious. There's nothing wrong with that. If you have a difficult time putting yourself in your customers' shoes, then let them help you into their shoes—and let your honest, needs-seeking questions be the shoe horn. Let me share a personal experience with a salesperson who did this successfully, despite her company's initial mistakes.

> **People like Bill sell well because they treat their customers like real people instead of a piece of meat.**

One of the most important dates during the year is my wife's birthday. Among many of her surprises in 2003, I decided to start the day by having a single red rose and twelve Mylar "Happy Birthday" balloons (her favorites) delivered to our door. I placed the order with the company 1-800-FLOWERS and asked for the bouquet to be delivered the morning of her birthday.

When I arrived home the afternoon *before* her special day, my wife surprised me when she thanked me for the wonderful balloons. I kissed her and told her she was welcome, and then we went on with our evening, never really discussing that the balloons were a day early. As we were getting ready to go to bed, I glanced at the balloons and flower on her nightstand. I noticed that the bouquet looked a little light in the balloon category so I quickly counted them. Sure enough, there were only six balloons. I was going to let the day-early delivery slide. But when I realized that the bouquet was also short six balloons, I had a problem.

The following morning I called 1-800-FLOWERS, and the woman on the other end professionally and enthusiastically introduced herself as Connor. I was immediately aware that she was ready to help. I explained the situation to her, and without missing a beat she said, "Mr. Duncan, that is completely unacceptable. It's not the way we do business, and I take full responsibility from this point forward in making sure we not only meet, but exceed your expectations." She wasted no time putting herself in my shoes.

Connor continued asking questions to empathize even more. "Mr. Duncan," she said, "tell me what needs to happen so that you will feel good about your choice of us as your special occasions provider."

"Well," I replied, "I don't want to pay for something that I didn't get, and to be honest, I'm annoyed that the order was sent a day early."

"I'll tell you what," she said. "You *shouldn't* have to pay for what you didn't get. I am setting up a refund right now for six of the balloons since you didn't get those. And because we delivered them a day early, we'd like to pay for your next special occasion delivery. Are there any other special occasions coming up?"

"Yes," I replied. "Valentine's Day."

Connor then asked what I'd like to do, and I told her. "Done!" she stated with confidence. But she didn't stop there.

After completing the order in her computer, Connor asked if I was completely satisfied. She didn't assume a thing. When I said yes, I was satisfied, she asked for my permission to arrange for the next two sales at no obligation to me. She explained that if I would simply give her my e-mail address, she would send me an automatic reminder next year on the two dates I had chosen, and at that time she would love the privilege of doing business with me again. I, of course, was happy to give my permission. And because Connor understood the importance of putting herself in my shoes and empathizing with me, she will not only have my unsolicited business each year, she has also been referred to you and every other person who reads this book. When begging is not an option, your selling options are virtually unlimited.

BUSINESS MADE EASY

Before we move on to the last two chapters, I want to make sure you're clear on how to put an end to begging. To take your selling actions to a legitimate, lucrative level, you need to remember that your goal as a salesperson is to *make doing business with you easy.* That's it. That's the bottom line. In the process of employing the five principles we've discussed, your goal is never to make customers work to buy from you. Never make prospects earn your business. You earn theirs. It's your job to make "yes" the most logical, natural response of your prospects. And it's really not that difficult when it's just a matter of treating your customers the way you'd expect to be treated if you were on the other side of your desk or the other end of your phone. I'll let you in on a little secret that I use to gauge my success with prospects and to avoid for good the mistake of begging. Before, during, and after a selling transaction, I inevitably ask myself: *Would I buy from me?* And if my answer is yes, I know that I'm doing my best to earn my prospects' buy-in and subsequently their business. And the same will be true for you.

CHAPTER NINE

Mistake #9: Skimming

*Focusing on surface profitability instead of
client satisfaction*

Since every twenty-third person in the U.S. is a salesperson, we can say with a high degree of certainty that the sales profession is very competitive. But I bet you already knew that. If you're like most salespeople, you probably don't have to look beyond the walls of your own company to find good competition—sometimes of the friendly variety, other times of the antagonistic variety. In fact, you may even have to compete for your job on a regular basis. Simply put, selling competition is everywhere.

And the truth is that even if you begin selling an innovative product, you can be sure that you won't be the only one selling it for long. Soon others will have something similar to sell. That's just how it works, isn't it? Once a product gains popularity, other entrepreneurs will create similar products of their own. We see this every year. One car company begins selling an SUV or a minivan, then every car company follows suit—some sooner than others, but eventually everyone is selling a similar type of vehicle because people are buying. Or one clothing designer comes up with a certain type of shoe—and it sells like crazy. Then before you can say high heel, every other designer from Milan to Miami is selling a similar shoe.

Everyone wants a piece of the pie—sellers and buyers alike—especially when the pie is selling like hotcakes. And do you know what that means?

It means that no matter what you're selling or for whom you're selling, to be perpetually successful in the sales profession, you must win customers from the competition initially, and you must win customers from the competition incessantly. Salespeople who focus only on customer *acquisition* don't remain on top for long. It's those with high customer *retention* who rule the roost. And that's where many salespeople go wrong. They put all their efforts into acquiring customers—and that's certainly important—but they fall short when it comes to retaining customers for the long haul. It's a fatal mistake I call "skimming." And if you don't do away with it in your sales career, your sales success will eventually dry up.

> **Salespeople who focus only on customer acquisition don't remain on top for long.**

DIGGING AND NOT DRINKING

The mistake of skimming is essentially putting all your eggs into the acquisition basket and, contrary to Andrew Carnegie's age-old advice, *not* watching the basket. Skimming is pulling out all the stops to establish a relationship with a customer, then bailing out on the marriage. It's doing all that needs to be done to earn a sale, then doing nothing to keep a client. And unless you enjoy working harder than you have to, prospecting more than you need to, and maintaining a high level of stress and instability in your sales career, then you must do something to avoid the mistake of skimming.

The results of skimming aren't always immediately measurable. Many sales skimmers launch out of the starting gate with a great selling strategy and end up with a ton of business right away. And that's a good thing . . . at first. But what they soon learn—usually one client at a time—is that getting sales is only digging the well to sales success. Keeping clients is the spring that fills the well. And therefore, shallow, untapped relationships eventually leave one's sales career high and dry. Robert is one salesperson who found this out a little late.

When Robert started out as a pharmaceutical sales rep, he already knew how to gain a prospect's trust and close sales. He was a well-spoken, confident man, a good listener, and a genuine communicator. He seemed to have all the tools to be highly successful in any sales job. But he chose the pharmaceutical industry because he believed that the profits loomed large. And he was right. In fact, in his first year on the job, he closed 14 percent more sales than anyone else in his company. As a result, he cleared $100,000 in income in his first year—a feat that only one other salesperson had ever accomplished in the history of the company. Needless to say, Robert was riding high and ready to rock and roll in his second year. He expected even bigger things, but something happened that he didn't expect.

When Robert entered his second year, he had a simple strategy: spend 25 percent of his time acquiring new clients and the rest of his time reaping repeat business from the previous year's clients. But there was only one problem with his strategy—and it was a big one. He hadn't really kept in touch with the clients to whom he'd sold the previous year. Aside from a thank-you letter and one follow-up call to each of them to make sure their orders were fulfilled as requested, Robert hadn't been in touch at all. Sure, he had earned their trust enough to win their business once—but when he went back to them for a second go-around, many of them had moved on.

One by one, Robert paid visits to his clients from the previous year, and one by one, they told him that they had already been scooped up by another rep from another firm. It wasn't that they didn't like Robert. It was that he wasn't around when they had needs—and someone else was. Since Robert knew that his customers placed orders for his product on an annual basis, he just assumed that the clients he'd won in his first year would want refills one year from the date he initially sold to them. But he was wrong in his assumption. Many of his first-year clients placed their orders at the beginning of the fiscal year and others at the beginning of the calendar year. And then there were others who needed more of his product in less than a year. But Robert was out of touch.

At the six-month mark of his second year, Robert had not even closed one-third of the sales he had made the prior year. Furthermore, of those to whom he had sold in the previous year, only a meager 15 percent had given him repeat business. As a result, he was forced to go back to the drawing board in the hopes of salvaging what was shaping up to be a very mediocre year of selling.

For the remainder of his second year, Robert went back to selling the way he had in the beginning, spending most of his time prospecting for new business. That, he hoped, would keep him atop his company's salesperson charts when the year ended. But despite his efforts to return to his first-year form, Robert ended up near the middle of the pack. When the end-of-the-year results were reported for his second year, he had fallen from the top salesperson spot to thirteenth. Not only that, Robert's income had nearly been cut in half, and his hours on the job had increased significantly in an effort to make up for his lost business. Being out of touch with his clients had cost Robert in more ways than one. And the same holds true for most sales professionals.

The truth is that many ambitious salespeople learn about the fatal mistake of skimming the same way Robert did. They do a great job of acquiring a client base, but because they fail to retain clients in a proactive manner, they have to rely heavily on prospecting to sustain their success. And when the market slows or becomes over-saturated or clients' needs take an unexpected turn, such salespeople have a tough time maintaining anything more than mediocre success. Ultimately, skimming salespeople learn this lesson: productive prospecting can take you only so far in the world of sales. While it's a vital part of any profitable selling strategy, it can only open the door to sales success. Productive prospecting doesn't guarantee that the door of success will remain open.

SUBTRACTING SUCCESS

To be a successful sales professional, you must *establish* trust with your prospects so that they become clients. You must also *foster* their trust so that they remain clients. And if you don't, you're not only staking your entire sales career on a consistent influx of new business—on constant prospecting—but you're never tapping the full potential of your relationships. When you make the mistake of skimming, you may as well write your competition a check every month because you're losing money on a regular basis by not retaining the clients you've landed. You're subtracting success. You're losing repeat and referral business that *was* in your hands . . . if only you'd held tightly to what you had earned. Consider the lifetime value of clients in two common sales industries.

THE REAL ESTATE CLIENT

A. The average commission amount $6,000

B. Average number of commissions/
   year from one client   .25 (or 1 in every 4 years)

C. Revenue per year (A x B) $1,500

D. Client life cycle   20 years

E. Client value over life cycle (C x D) $30,000

Indirect Value

F. Average client referrals per year   4

G. Potential value of client referrals
   in your 1st year $6,000

H. Revenue if 1st-year referrals close
   and reach life cycle $120,000

Total Lifetime Value of One Real
Estate Client (E + H) $150,000

THE AUTO CLIENT

A. The average commission amount $1,000

B. Number of sales per year from
   one client   .33 (or 1 every 3 years)

C. Revenue per year (A x B) $330

D. Client life cycle   20 years

E. Client value over life cycle (C x D) $6,600

Indirect/Word-of-mouth Value

F. Average client referrals per year   4

164

G. Potential value of client
referrals per year $1,320

H. Revenue if 1st-year referrals close
and reach life cycle $26,400

Total Lifetime Value of
One Auto Client (E + H) $33,000

As you can see, when you make the mistake of skimming with your client relationships, you end up forfeiting a lot of money over the long haul. And those numbers reflect only the amount of business you would lose from *one* client. Can you imagine how much more money you would lose if you skimmed with multiple client relationships?

- Skimming with 10 high-end real estate client relationships in 1 year would amount to *$1,500,000 lost* over 20 years.

- Skimming with 10 average auto client relationships in 1 year would amount to *$330,000 lost* over 20 years.

We're not talking about losing a few bucks here and there. We're talking about losing your retirement. The mistake of skimming can cost you big time. It's one thing to rely heavily on prospecting to keep your sales business alive—although that's reason enough to avoid the mistake of skimming because it's an inefficient business practice. When you also consider that skimming is essentially writing off thousands of dollars every year to your competition, making the mistake starts to look more like negligence. Essentially it's helping your competition beat you. It's doing all the work to beat your competition, but always forfeiting the victory. A salesperson who does everything right to earn a client's trust and then disregards the relationship is like a guy who courts a girl and then leaves her at the altar. The only difference, however, is that in the world of sales the one who gets hurt is the one doing the leaving.

WHAT'S YOUR SHARE?

Foundationally, salespeople who make the mistake of skimming do so because they rely on what's called a "market-share" mentality instead of a "client-share" mentality.

Let's say that over the course of a month, there are one hundred sales in your given territory that are available to you and your competitors. If you landed five of those available sales, then you'd end up with a 5 percent market share for the month . . .

Closed 5 of 100 sales available in your market = 5 percent market share

Generally speaking, to maximize your market share, you must sell your product to as many clients as you possibly can in a given market—the greater the number of clients you have, the higher your market share. But the problem is that usually means spending a lot less time with a lot more people. In effect, to increase your market share, you have to spread yourself thinner, which results in shallow, untapped relationships and a very unstable business foundation.

On the other hand, if you were striving to increase your client share, you would focus on fostering deeper relationships with fewer people—spreading yourself thicker, so to speak. Following the example just given: if in the same one-month period you focused on only two clients who offered the potential of ten sales (directly through the clients themselves or indirectly through their referrals), and you secured half of them, you would end up with a 50 percent client-share . . .

Closed 5 of 10 sales available from 2 clients = 50 percent client-share

And here's the beauty of this strategy: while you still closed the same net amount of sales as in the previous example (five), it undoubtedly required much less effort because the clients already trusted you. You didn't have to do any prospecting to secure your sales. In essence, you let your existing clients prospect for you. Now, I don't know about you, but spending highly productive time with clients who know me sounds much better than pounding the pavement or the phone pad unendingly for the purpose of spending highly unproductive time with prospects who don't know me from Adam. And I have a sense you feel the same way.

The easiest way to understand the skimming concept of market share is to think of it as a horizontal selling strategy. Take a look:

MARKET-SHARE MENTALITY:
Increasing new client base equals success.

Taken at face value, increasing your market share seems to be a perfectly logical strategy; after all, you *do* increase your sales when you increase your number of clients in a given market. But when you dig deeper, you begin to see how a market-share mentality can lead to more strife than success.

First, a growth strategy based on your market-share numbers forces you to rely on a constant influx of new clients as the bare minimum for success. That's not only hard work; it's expensive. With a higher marketing overhead and a much greater time investment, acquiring new business always costs more than reaping repeat and referral business. Furthermore, when you make new client acquisition a requirement to stay afloat, you voluntarily put yourself in a pressure cooker where you must rely on people you don't know yet for success. Of course, that may be a requirement if you're just starting off, but it's certainly not a necessity when you've been in business for more than a year or two.

The second problem with a market-share mentality is that it doesn't take into account the full value of your clients. As you saw earlier, new clients don't reach full value unless you retain them for the long haul. But a market-share mentality would implore you to put current clients on the shelf in order to spend the majority of your time acquiring new clients (remember that having more clients equals a higher market share). In effect, a market-share mentality implores you to spread yourself thinner—to only skim the initial business from client relationships and then move on—in order to increase your success. But what ultimately result are shallow, untapped relationships and a very unstable business foundation.

On the other hand, if you were striving to increase your client share, you wouldn't run into these unenviable problems. Furthermore, you'd have a heck of a lot less stress.

CLIENT-SHARE MENTALITY: Increasing current client business equals success.

A salesperson who focuses on increasing client share strives to tap the full value of every client he or she obtains. He is less concerned about increasing his client base because he understands that once he has earned trust with a client, seeking repeat and referral business from that client is always more efficient and productive than acquiring business from new clients in the market. In essence, a client-share mentality is a vertical approach to selling that has as its primary focus *deepening* the potential of every sales relationship. As a result, prospecting for new business eventually becomes more an option than a requirement. And as you can see, it's certainly the better strategy when it comes to improving your sales business:

MARKET-SHARE MENTALITY	CLIENT-SHARE MENTALITY
You rely on new business.	You rely on repeat and referral business.
New clients are main income source.	Existing clients are main income source.

Marketing is required.	Marketing becomes obsolete.
Prospecting is required.	Prospecting is optional.
Time investment remains high.	Time investment steadily decreases.
Stress remains high.	Stress steadily decreases.
You must sell clients.	Clients sell you.

When all the factors are laid bare, a market-share mentality is an expensive, perpetually stressful, inefficient selling strategy. It causes you to skim in your client relationships in order to acquire more clients. But that strategy makes it very difficult for you to create momentum. Sure, you may hone your selling skills and become really good at closing sales, but the truth is that no matter how good you are, when you make the mistake of skimming, your success is still reliant on other people—namely, clients to whom you haven't yet sold a thing.

On the other hand, when you take a client-share approach to success, you create momentum without a reliance on prospecting, and you decrease your overhead and the time you have to spend closing sales. That's because the salesperson who puts her confidence in a client-share strategy knows that clients who trust her can sell her better than she can sell herself.

FROM SOLO TO SYMPHONY

Avoiding the mistake of skimming in your relationships is a matter of moving your business from a reliance on prospecting to a reliance on partnering. In other words, to stop skimming in your sales career, you must begin moving your existing client relationships from a buyer-seller affiliation to a partnership that's governed by give-and-take.

When you make the mistake of skimming, *you* alone are your only source of sales. Consequently success is a solo effort. And while you may be the best and most trusted closer in your industry (remember Robert from the beginning of the chapter), until you tap into the resource of others—namely, your existing clients—you will find that your sales success is either short-lived or very tough to sustain. In contrast, the salespeople who are perpetually on top know that it takes a selling symphony to create a never-ending crescendo of sales success—salespeople like Jim McMahan and Mary Harker.

When Jim met Mary for the first time in 1987, he had been in the mortgage loan business for a mere six months. But don't be fooled. Jim knew what he was doing better than most sales freshmen. He had spent some time working under the wings of Zig Ziglar and understood that salesmanship was much more than client numbers. He knew it took solid client relationships to build a foundation for lasting success. Sure, he was only a baby in the mortgage industry working his second sales job—while Mary, on the other hand, had seventeen years of experience as a top-notch real estate broker. But despite the disparity in experience, Jim knew right away that Mary was a good fit for his business. And ironically, it was because Mary understood the value of going deeper in relationships as well.

When Jim called Mary for the first time in an effort to begin establishing a trust-based relationship, he mentioned that he and his wife had their first baby on the way. Mary was thrilled. She asked more questions for which she genuinely wanted to know the answers. Questions about Jim, about his wife, about their little bun in the oven, about their future and their values. Mary, Jim learned, was just as passionate about family as he was. Furthermore, she shared the same order of values: God first, family second, business third. If he wasn't sure going into the prospecting call, Jim was certain now: Mary would be a huge asset to his business; and he hoped that he could prove that he would be valuable to her.

Although Mary wasn't a prospect in the typical sense of the term in that she wouldn't be the one directly purchasing loans from him, Jim knew that Mary must be treated as a potential client from the beginning. After all, she was the gatekeeper to many great clients who were buying homes—and Jim could offer each of them their home loans. As Jim saw it, he was not only selling himself and his services to Mary, he was selling to her clients as well. Jim just needed to show Mary that his services and their relationship would be mutually beneficial—as beneficial for her and her clients as it would be for him. Jim knew he and Mary could be good friends. And he felt that he had established trust with her in their first phone call. But building high trust that leads to lasting success means going deeper than a mere friendship. As a result, Jim knew he had to invest more. He had to go deeper with Mary if his relationship with her was going to reap a full harvest.

Jim began to contact Mary on a regular basis. Always to build more trust and share in friendship. And most times to share his vision for their partnership as well. He knew that Mary was a busy lady with many demands on her time. And he knew that she strived for excellence in everything she did—in fact, that's why she was one of the top real estate brokers in the nation. Therefore, what he had to offer Mary needed to meet her high standards; and it needed to fit her values as well.

It took a full year of fostering trust with her and casting a clear, concise vision to her before Mary began giving Jim business. But

Jim's persistence and consistency paid off. In fact, every month Jim now closes an average of three to four loans for clients whom Mary has shared with him. What's more, of the 3,000 clients in Jim's current database, Mary is responsible for 20 percent of them. The quick-sell, quick-money, short-term relationship strategy is actually the hardest road you can take as a sales professional. Fortunately for him, Jim understood that from the beginning, and now he's arranged more than $750 million in financing for more than 4,000 families over the past 17 years. And if you desire similar success, you must move away from a skimming strategy in your sales efforts to one that fosters long-term partnerships.

It's not difficult. Forming strategic sales partnerships like Jim and Mary have is simply seeking agreeable terms for mutually beneficial relationships each time you acquire a new client. And you must do the same if you desire to move your sales relationships away from skimming.

CONDUCTING A SELLING SYMPHONY

To transition your existing clients into productive partners and create your own symphony of sales success, you must take five steps. As you consider each of the following steps, keep in mind that this system is not only meant to be applied to every client you have now; it's also meant to be applied to every client you will have in the future.

STEP 1: TAKE INVENTORY.

Determine your existing clients' value. Who are your lead players—your clients who can give you loads of their own business and also lots of referral business? Who are your accompanying players—your clients who may not provide you with big business, but who can provide you with consistent business in the form of repeat or referral sales? And which players don't make the cut? These are your clients who are either high maintenance or low profit or both.

You're the conductor of this symphony, so only you can define who is fit to play and who isn't. But the bottom line is that you want to invest the majority of your time in clients who will perform well and on a consistent basis—in other words, clients whose business and referrals you can rely on. Therefore, if you have clients who don't fit that bill, it's in your best interest to cut them to make room for clients who do.

Jim didn't have many clients when he met Mary. But he knew a quality potential client when he saw it. Jim knew Mary was a major player in the real estate industry from the get-go. Her perpetual success and her clients' satisfaction spoke for themselves. And once Jim realized that Mary shared his same values and was open to the value of a deeper relationship, he placed her at the top of his prospecting list.

STEP 2: DETERMINE YOUR INVESTMENT LEVELS.

Once you know which clients can be lead players and which can provide consistent accompaniment to your sales business, you must then determine how much time and money you will invest in each of them in order to sustain their business and tap their resources. There is no magic formula to how much you should invest. Like any monetary investment, you just need to consider your potential return from each client on your list. Typically, where money is concerned, my firm invests about 15 percent of our top clients' value back into them. In other words, if a client is worth $20,000 a year to our firm, we will invest about $3,000 back into that client every year in the form of special benefits, privileges, gifts, and discounts. For an accompanying client who is worth about $5,000 a year to our firm, we will invest about 10 percent or $500 back into him or her each year. You get the picture. And following this example, you must do the same with your time investment. Where time is concerned, Jim and Mary meet once a quarter for a few hours to talk about any changes in their visions, values, strategy, or plans. They don't need much more time than that nowadays because they know each other and each others' business so well. Their families get together once every few months to just relax and have fun. They share sorrows and joys, prayer requests and praises. The truth is that they have built such a solid, trustworthy relationship in the business sense that they share much more than business success with each other. They share in each others' life success as well.

STEP 3: CAST YOUR VISION TO YOUR CLIENTS.

On an individual basis, schedule meetings with each of your clients who made the cut in the first step. Don't cast your vision on the phone, but explain to them that they are vital to the ongoing success of your business and you'd like to discuss the feasibility of forming a mutually beneficial partnership where you offer them discounts and special privileges in exchange for their repeat business and referrals. Then in your formal meeting, take the following approach:

- First and foremost, let them know how much you appreciate their business and desire to continue serving them in the most valuable way possible by developing and fostering a mutually beneficial partnership.

- Second, share how *you* desire to add value to *them*—with their direction—in the form of . . .
  - → money invested in them (discounts, referral incentives).
  - → time invested in the relationship (formal and informal

      meetings to foster the relationship and remain in touch with changing needs and desires).

→ valuable benefits that can be determined by them (a special phone number to get in touch with you easily, a first-priority status on all orders).

→ miscellaneous gifts (dinner on you once a quarter, tickets to sporting events, movie or theater passes).

- Third, ask them to help you determine how the two of you can compose an arrangement for a mutually beneficial relationship—a symphony.

Keep in mind that this step doesn't work very well if you haven't already established trust with a client or if, like Robert the pharmaceutical rep, you've been out of touch for a while. In such cases, you may need to establish a level of consistency and integrity with your client before you take this third step. If that's the case, I recommend spending six to twelve months carrying out Step 2 with a client before you move to Step 3. That's precisely what Jim did as he built trust in his relationship with Mary. Since he didn't have an established relationship with her, he began by sharing with her his appreciation for her high level of excellence in her endeavors. Furthermore, he was honest from the start. In sharing his vision with her, he didn't promise more than he knew he could deliver. He simply told her that he was committed to helping her lead people down the path that was right for them—not merely right for his business. In doing so Jim conveyed to Mary that he shared her same values and that her clients would be in good hands with him. Eventually, Mary began to see firsthand that Jim was more interested in doing what's best for his clients when he sent one of his clients to a competitor who offered a better loan. And by the way, that's something

Jim has done many more times since then—and Mary understands completely.

STEP 4: ORCHESTRATE WHAT PARTS THEY WILL PLAY.

Obviously, you will want your best clients playing the biggest part in helping you succeed. So once you've established your part in adding value to your clients, your next step—with their help—is to determine what parts they will play in your relationships' arrangement in order to further your business. There are three things you need to determine:

The amount of business you will receive from them on an annual basis. Remember that if this is a partnership that they have agreed to, it is expected that they look to you for your particular product or service on a regular basis . . . unless you cannot fulfill your end of the bargain.

The number of referrals you will receive from them on an annual basis. Some clients will have a natural stream of referrals that they can pass to you per your arrangement, and tapping into that stream can be very valuable for your business. For example, if you are a home loan originator and your client works for a construction firm, he would come across a constant influx of people needing new home loans or refinancing for a remodel. Other clients may not have this sort of advantage, and that's okay.

How they will help you recruit new clients if and when it is necessary. If certain clients don't have a way to pass you referrals on a regular basis, determine how they can make your prospecting efforts much easier. While prospecting will undoubtedly become your secondary method of seeking business once a few partnerships are orchestrated, it's wise to have a highly effective plan ready to go when you do need to prospect. And that's where your client/partners can come in very handy. Remember that clients who trust you can sell you much better than you can sell yourself. Social proof is an invaluable tool in sales, and when clients are your partners you can maximize its use. The easiest way to do this is by simply composing an arrangement like Jim and Mary have. According to Jim, one of the main reasons he and Mary's relationship is so successful is that they have always relied on their ability to cross-sell each other. When they were working out the initial strategy of their partnership, they simply composed a script that each agreed to adhere to (in informal fashion), which essentially increased the credibility of the other partner. For example, when Mary is in the process of selling a home to a client, she simply asks about their financing and then tells them about Jim, her loan financing expert. When that client calls on Jim to seek his services, Jim truthfully assures the clients that they are working with the best real estate broker around. In doing this, they build each others' platform of trust and credibility with their shared clients as well as diffuse any hesitation the clients might have.

STEP 5: STRIKE UP THE BAND. LITERALLY.

The greatest partnership arrangement in the world isn't going to make a bit of difference in your selling career until you put your wand in motion. Not only must you begin playing out your determined partnership roles, you must do so on a regular basis in order to make certain that you don't become rusty and out of tune with each others' values, needs, and goals. And if you do so with integrity and the right motives, you may eventually end up with a successful business relationship like Jim and Mary's.

To skirt the skimming mistake in your sales career as Jim and Mary did, you must understand one thing: your greatest advantage over your selling competition is knowing your clients better than they do. And while there are no perfect formulas for composing a seamless selling symphony—because it's more art than science—as in any relationship, the better in tune you are with your clients' needs, the more readily you can meet their needs. And that way, when the competition comes knocking on your clients' doors, it won't be music to their ears.

CHAPTER TEN

Mistake #10: Stagnating

*Losing your sales edge by neglecting
your growth curve*

A survey conducted by market research company Crestwood Associates revealed that nearly two-thirds of sales customers continue to look for and purchase products from other vendors despite receiving the level of value and service they expected from their current vendor.[1] This statistic indicates that in the world of sales, simply meeting customers' expectations is good enough to secure a client, but not necessarily to keep a client.

In an era of ever-expanding choices, being successful in the sales profession takes more than courtesy and kindness. It takes more than mere professionalism. And it takes more than merely meeting customers' needs. Yet many salespeople are still selling with a simple arsenal of service, value, and good products. And while those things are integral parts of being a successful salesperson (in other words, you can't be successful without them), they are not enough to set you apart from your competition in the long run. In short, service, value, and good products can earn you the trust of your clients, but these things will not necessarily keep your clients loyal in the long run because smart consumers always have wandering eyes, searching for better deals.

Other salespeople who are striving to improve their game are *also* taking steps to increase their level of service, add more value, and improve their products. And other ambitious salespeople are seeking the same advice you are—from the same authors, speakers, and sales sages. Your toughest competitors are hearing the same tips, reading the same bestsellers, and listening to the same motivational merchandise. (And they're probably reading this page along with you.) And because that's the case, yesterday's sales advice is today's standard of business.

For example, in the early 1990s we were all talking about offering a Nordstrom level of customer service in order to be successful. But before long, many sales companies and individuals boasted the same level of service, and Nordstrom was having to claw for consumers' loyalty. More choices that looked a lot like Nordstrom cropped up, and as a result, their customers began straying. As a result, Nordstrom's sales suffered. An April 19, 1999, *Business Week* article titled "Great Service Wasn't Enough" discussed Nordstrom's subpar sales growth and lower-than-expected profits. The article claimed that overexpansion had hurt Nordstrom's numbers and subsequently its claim to fame. But William E. Nordstrom put it this way: "We have not been able to keep up with the changing needs of the customers."[2]

All this doesn't mean that the Nordstrom standard of selling is futile. It certainly isn't. In fact, winning customers' trust is about maintaining a certain high standard of selling, and Nordstrom still does it well. But so do other department stores and retail chains. And once your competition maintains the same standard of selling, you must *raise* your standard in order to keep your customers loyal to you and you alone. And that's where Nordstrom went wrong. That's where many salespeople go wrong. They expect that what won their clients' trust yesterday will keep them loyal today. It's a fatal mistake I call "stagnating," and if you make it long enough, your competition will eventually swallow up your best clients. A real estate salesperson named John learned this the hard way.

> **Yesterday's sales advice is today's standard of business.**

John was at the top of his selling game. As a real estate broker, he'd literally taken over the market in his city by offering a high level of customer service to those who brought business his way. He'd accounted for about 55 percent of his employer's business for two years running. But about midway through the year 2000, things began to change—namely, his clients' allegiance.

John's main competition had always come from another broker named Lisa. And while John had managed to outsell her for three years in a row, Lisa's stock was beginning to rise in the minds not only of her clients, but also of John's. She was providing the same level of service that John was, but she was also building deeper relationships and offering generous referral incentives to clients who referred her to others interested in buying or selling a home. And slowly but surely she became a household name in the home industry.

John had made a name for himself in the mid-1990s as the courteous, servant salesperson who would bend over backward for you. He was known as the real estate broker who would "bring your home to you." But his uniqueness was no longer a surprise. Lisa was also one who would go the extra mile to serve her customers, and so were others in that area. John had set the service standard with his house calls, his over-the-top chauffeur service to and from home sites, and his keen ability to make customers' home-buying process as easy as ordering a house from a catalog.

But by the year 2001, John's service standard had become commonplace in the industry. People could get his level of service from a number of top real estate brokers in the area. Like John, many of his competitors were also delivering all paperwork to and from customers' homes, offering complimentary chauffeur services to take customers to home sites, and finding ways to make the home-buying process seamless and as easy as 1-2-3. In essence, John's competition was rising up to him, but he wasn't raising the bar. And eventually someone else came along and set a new bar—and that someone was Lisa.

Lisa became the salesperson who provided top-notch service and a down-home experience during a time when consumers were increasingly skeptical about spending money. Sure, she would bend over backward for you. But she also wanted to get to know you personally. She was known for taking clients to lunch or having them over to a Southern home-cooked meal—without ever speaking a word about past or future business. In that manner, she attracted many people who were clients of her competition. Lisa strategically became the real estate broker who was "genuinely looking out for her customers' best interests." In a competitive industry and a tight economy, she managed to set herself apart from the rest.

But John didn't clue in until he heard that one of his best clients was "shopping around" for someone to help his brother sell his home. When John asked his client what he needed to do to win his brother's business, the client replied, "I don't think you can do anything at this point. My brother and his wife had dinner with another broker last night. I think they're gonna use her."

In the end, John did manage to win the brother's business by cutting his commission in half (something I don't recommend you do because it cheapens your business and lowers your credibility with other clients). But taking that step didn't keep John atop his industry. His selling strategy had been stagnant for too long. And as a result, by February 2002 Lisa had overtaken John as the top salesperson in their city—an honor she still holds today. John, incidentally, is currently a distant number four.

A SELLING CESSPOOL

What John had to learn the hard way is something many salespeople never learn—that what got a client to buy yesterday will not necessarily win a client today. And as a result, many salespeople end up lagging behind in new sales or losing longtime clients to the cutting-edge competition. But it's the inevitable result of our final fatal mistake called "stagnating."

Salespeople who make the mistake of stagnating are out of touch with their clients and their sales climate. But unlike our previous mistake of skimming, stagnating is not really a mistake of negligence. It is better classified as a mistake of naiveté. Stagnating is not failing to retain clients because of a lack of investment in the relationships. It's a failure to gain and retain clients because of a lack of professional growth and discernment. Stagnating is losing your selling edge through sluggish growth or slow insight. *It's using a static sales strategy in a dynamic industry.* It's assuming the selling climate in your industry hasn't changed in months and then setting sail on the ever-changing, unforgiving sales seas. And when you make the mistake of stagnating, you usually end up getting blown out of the water by the more savvy and forward-moving competition.

In the sales profession, many factors shift on a regular basis. And at the top of the list is consumer choice. In their book *Differentiate or Die* (John Wiley & Sons, 2000), Jack Trout and Steve Rivkin discuss the "explosion of choice" that has bombarded consumers in the U.S. between the 1970s and 1990s. The authors offer the following eye-opening chart that vividly illustrates how consumers' buying choices in numerous sales industries have literally exploded—and have continued to grow—since the early 1970s.

ITEM	EARLY 1970s	LATE 1990s
Vehicle models	140	260
KFC menu items	7	14
Vehicle styles	654	1,212
Frito-Lay chip varieties	10	78
SUV styles	8	38
Breakfast cereals	160	340
PC models	0	400
Pop-Tarts	3	29
Software titles	0	250,000
Soft drink brands	20	87
Websites	0	4,757,894
Bottled water brands	16	50
Movie releases	267	458
Milk types	4	19
Airports	11,261	18,202
Colgate toothpastes	2	17
Magazine titles	339	790
Mouthwashes	15	66
New book titles	40,530	77,446
Dental flosses	12	64
Community colleges	886	1,742
Prescription drugs	6,131	7,563
Amusement parks	362	1,174
OTC pain relievers	17	141
TV screen sizes	5	15
Levi's jean styles	41	70

Houston TV channels	5	185
Running shoe styles	5	285
Radio stations	7,038	12,458
Women's hosiery styles	5	90
McDonald's items	13	43
Contact lens types	1	36

From *Differentiate or Die*, "The Explosion of Choice," by Jack Trout and Steve Rivkin (John Wiley & Sons, 2000). Reprinted by permission of John Wiley & Sons, Inc.

In their concluding remarks on the explosion of consumer choice, Trout and Rivkin write the following:

> The dictionary defines tyranny as absolute power that often is harsh or cruel. So it is with choice. With the enormous competition, markets today are driven by choice. The customer has so many good alternatives that you pay dearly for your mistakes. Your competitors get your business and you don't get it back very easily. Companies that don't understand this will not survive.[3]

And I'd add that the same holds true for the salespeople of such companies. The fact is that when you make the mistake of stagnating, when you allow your selling strategy to grow old and stale in an ever-growing, ever-changing industry, you will end up a bottom dweller in your own cesspool of lost sales.

THE NORMALCY OF CHANGE

Many things change in the sales industry on a regular basis. And if you don't adjust your selling strategy along with the changes, if you don't continue to raise your own selling bar, you will end up stuck in the mud while your competition glides by you. Here's what I'm talking about:

PRODUCTS CHANGE.

Take MP3 players, for example. Before the legal actions of musicians and their labels tamed Napster, MP3 players were the latest craze. Selling them was a cinch. You buy this microsized Walkman for about the price of five CDs and then download hours and hours of all the free music you want from the Internet. Voilá! At a fraction of the cost and time of a typical music collection, you could build an entire music library. But once Napster and its cyber-clones were told they couldn't offer the music downloads for free, MP3s lost popularity. Sure, people still buy them. But not for the same reasons they bought them before. And if you aren't coming up with a new approach to make MP3s attractive, you're probably not selling many.

CLIENTS CHANGE.

If you were a real estate sales professional in the mid-1990s, you might have noticed a big change in your clientele—especially if you lived in California. With the boom of the dot.com and computer technology came a much younger and richer brand of home buyer. Young men and women not far removed from high school started looking for million-dollar homes in which to invest their cyber-fortunes. They were a far cry from the typical clientele. And if you were still approaching the new breed of client with a stale selling strategy, you undoubtedly missed the boat.

CLIENTS' VALUES CHANGE.

Following the events of September 11, 2001, many people started to rethink what was most important to them. Sales suffered and continue to suffer in many industries because people just don't value what they once did. Or at least, they don't value certain things as much. Take a look at the changes in Americans' values prior to September 11, 2001, and then following that tragic day:

PRIOR TO 9/11	FOLLOWING 9/11
1. Career	1. Family
2. Heart	2. Heart
3. Wealth	3. God
4. Health	4. Health
5. Family	5. Country
6. Home	6. Home
7. God	7. Career
8. Country	8. Wealth

USA Today, "American Workers Rethink Priorities," 4 October 2001. Used by permission.

The fact is that if you aren't currently selling with the knowledge of how your clients' values may have changed over the past two years, you're probably reeling in a pool of sales misery.

CLIENTS' NEEDS CHANGE.

If you've been in computer sales for the past ten to twenty years, you've no doubt seen major changes in the needs of your clients. Ten years ago, just having a laptop was considered a luxury. Today, everyone has one. And as a result, clients want smaller laptops to lighten their traveling load . . . with bigger screens to ease their ocular strain . . . faster processors to get work done more efficiently . . . and bigger memory to allow them to conduct all their business in one place on one computer screen. If you're still trying to pawn off laptops as a luxury item with bells and whistles that nobody wants, you're way behind the times.

MARKETS CHANGE.

The telecommunications market has changed drastically over the last fifteen years. In the late 1980s, cell phones weren't yet a hot commodity, so the biggest war was over who had the best long-distance package. Now, that's just a small, ancillary scuffle. The real marketing war between telecommunications companies and their sales staffers is over cell phone service and reliability. More and more people are going to their cell phones as their main mode of communication for local and long-distance calls. The market is abuzz with phrases like "Can you hear me now?" and "That's m-life," promising fast, reliable service with a smile and a color screen, Web mobility, and voice-activated dialing to boot. And now that the courts have passed a law that allows consumers to keep their individual cell phone numbers when moving from one phone company to another, the market is ablaze with the latest, greatest reasons to use one company or the other. And amidst all this, if you're still trying to sell long-distance service as a premium, you're probably struggling to make any sales strides. In fact, you're probably standing still.

YOU CHANGE.

Do life changes affect the way you sell? You better believe it. When you're single, it's much easier to appeal to younger, single clientele. When you're married, that may change. Furthermore, when you have children, your set of circumstances and your values are entirely different from your days before children. As a result, not only does your ability to appeal to a different crowd change, the things you sell may not be as appealing to you. And that's an important point to consider. If your product has lost its luster with you, how do you expect to sell it to another person? The bottom line is that you are a part of your product. And when you sell, you're selling not only your product or service but also yourself. Therefore, as you change, so does your sales offering—whether you like it or not. For instance, if you are selling minivans as a single person, you will have a tough time empathizing with your typical customer's needs and values. If you're married with children, that will change—and so must your selling approach.

Stagnating is essentially selling the same way year after year with the naive assumption that nothing has changed. That your product or service hasn't changed. That the market hasn't changed. That your clients or potential clients haven't changed. That consumers' wants and needs and values haven't changed. That you haven't changed. But everything changes, all the time. Therefore, to overcome the fatal mistake of stagnating, so must you.

> **Everything changes, all the time. Therefore, to overcome the fatal mistake of stagnating, so must you.**

THE NECESSITY OF CHANGE

To avoid the stink of a stagnant sales career, you must learn to grow with change. In other words, you must learn to keep a finger on the pulse of the market (something we hear quite often) and on the pulse of your clients' needs and values, the pulse of your product or service, and your own pulse. It's a good thing you have so many fingers.

For the remainder of this book, I want to show you how to do away with stagnating and how to use an anti-stagnating strategy to ensure that you remain on top of your selling game now and in the years to come. Here are four steps that you must take in order to remain apprised of the constant changes in your sales industry and retain a lead on your selling competition:

1. STUDY YOUR PRODUCT LIKE A CONSUMER.

There are so many product and service choices for consumers these days that there is now an entire industry dedicated to helping consumers make the right choices. There are Fodor's travel guides, Zagat's restaurant guides, the Robb Report for your expensive choices, and *Consumer Reports* and *Consumer Digest* to help you with just about every other product or service choice under the sun. Of course, there are also the "top tens" of numerous other products or services every year in a number of popular magazines. All are dedicated to helping consumers make the perfect choice. And if you are to maintain a selling edge with your product, you must know what the consumer world is saying. Find the magazines or newsletters or books that provide surveys and guides about your particular type of product. Take a look at what they are telling your customers to buy. Read about the trends that are predicted for your product. Then do some shopping to determine how your competitors are positioning your product.

All these things will help you empathize with your customers' wants and needs, and they will also help you constantly position your product in a unique, relevant manner. And that's the point. Don't fill your head with quality research and then waste it. Use it to position your product in such a way that pleasantly surprises your customers every year.

When a client of mine named Stacey started out as a sales professional, his personal growth regimen entailed reading two books a year. Hardly an effort. Today, he remains apprised of his market and his product on a daily basis. Furthermore, he reads from twenty-four to thirty books a year on many topics relating to his personal and professional growth. Coincidentally, he's now a sales manager and coach at one of the top companies in his industry, leading his salespeople from an average of $600,000 per month in sales when he began in 1998 to $3 million per month in sales in 2003.

2. SURVEY YOUR CLIENTS REGULARLY.

In the last chapter, we discussed the importance of transitioning your current clients to partners who have a shared interest in your success. When you've taken steps to ensure that happens with each client, keeping abreast of any changes in their wants, needs, or values is easy. In fact, the most effective and surefire way to pick up on such changes is to have an ongoing relationship with them. You can't just send out a bunch of survey mailers and hope they get back to you. And by the way, when you meet with clients, have an agenda. Know what questions you must ask them on a regular basis in order to make certain that no values or needs fall through the cracks. Also, remember to always make it worth their while.

Here's the beauty to this step. When you regularly survey all your clients, you not only stay abreast of any changes in their individual wants, needs, and values, but you also stay on top of any "corporate" changes in the buying climate. In other words, with the results of purposeful surveys, you have specific information that helps you cater to individual desires, and you have general information with which you can foresee general buying trends and adjust your sales efforts accordingly.

For instance, if you keep up with the auto industry's new offerings each year, you've undoubtedly noticed the recent facelift that has taken place at the Japanese-based Nissan Motor Company with its cutting-edge, award-winning commercials and the release of its new 350Z, Murano, and Infiniti G35 sports coupe, in addition to revamped Maxima, Altima, and Infiniti Q45 models. And that's no accident. According to David Magee, author of *Turnaround: How Carlos Ghosn Saved Nissan*, in the late 1990s, Nissan Motor Company "struggled so badly . . . that many insiders feared its doors might close due to a lack of sustained profitability . . . Management once hailed as progressive and trend-setting [had become] a part of Japan's old-boy network, arrogant and oblivious to market changes and customer needs."[4]

Insert into this climate Carlos Ghosn, the company's new president and CEO. And subsequently insert the beginning of a major turnaround. A new manufacturing plant in Mississippi would reduce production time for new models, and an aggressive cost-cutting plan, which, according to Ghosn, took into primary account "the reduction of everything that is not value added for the customer." As far as Ghosn saw it, in the late 1990s Nissan had lost touch with its customers' needs by creating products that neither excited them nor created loyalty to the Nissan brand. But since 1999 and the implementation of Ghosn's cutting-edge, customer-concerned strategy, Nissan has had its most profitable years in the company's history, which includes raising annual volumes by $6 billion and, according to Magee, stopping "the string of consecutive years the company lost market share in Japan dead in its tracks at twenty-seven."[5]

3. PLAY THE MARKET.

What I mean by that is to become a buyer in your own market. If you sell anything, to remain ahead of your competition, you must understand what it's like to be a consumer of your product. As a salesperson you can only adjust your selling efforts based on what you observe from the selling end of the transaction. But you can't truly empathize with your buyers until you are one—otherwise your empathy is really just sympathy.

When I say become a buyer, I mean just that. I believe that every salesperson who is truly interested in understanding his buyers and remaining on the cutting edge of his industry must own at least one of the particular product he sells. I'm not suggesting that you buy your product every month and supplement your competitors' wallets. (And obviously if you're in the auto or home or any high-end product industry, this isn't feasible.) But I am suggesting that to fully comprehend what a consumer of your particular product goes through in the process of buying and owning, you must have gone through the process at least once.

If it makes sense, make a habit of buying your particular product from different competitors (so that you don't give all your business to one) on a quarterly basis. If it's not financially possible to buy your product on a regular basis, then at least shop around every month. Immerse yourself in the buying process as much as you can.

4. SURVEY YOURSELF ANNUALLY.

Something I've practiced and preached for years now is what I call the "Annual Review with You." And it's geared to ensure that your needs and values in life are consistently met and upheld over the course of your selling career. In essence, it's designed to ensure that your life doesn't become stagnant in your pursuit of selling success. Dorothy

Canfield Fisher once said, "If we would only give the same amount of reflection to what we want to get out of life that we give to the question of what to do with a two weeks' vacation, we would be startled at our false standards and the aimless procession of our days."

To make certain that your cutting-edge selling pursuits don't cause your life to grow stale, begin conducting an annual review of your life's procession. Personally, I find a place of solitude free from distraction and spend no less than eight hours answering the following questions:

- What am I passionate about that gives meaning to my life?

- What do I value that gives me true satisfaction?

- Am I missing anything in my life right now that is important to me?

- Where do I want to be and what do I want to be doing in five, ten, and twenty years?

- What gifts has God given me that I am perfecting? Which gifts am I not using effectively?

- What would I be willing to die for?

- What is it about my job that makes me feel trapped? How can I change that?

- With regard to money, how much is enough? If I have more than enough, what purpose does the excess serve?

- Am I living a balanced life? Which areas need more time or focus?

- Where am I seeking inspiration, mentors, and working models to achieve greater significance?

- What do I want to be remembered for? Am I currently known for those things?

- What legacy do I want to leave my children? Am I leaving it?

"A man," said Samuel Johnson, "loves to review his mind."[6] And while this is true, it's not the purpose of conducting an annual review. The Annual Review with You is for the purpose of reviewing your heart, your soul. And when you do that on a yearly basis, you will ensure that nothing—not even sales success—will get in the way of the most important things in your life. And that's vital because selling success and life satisfaction can and should go hand in hand. And when they do, your competitors don't have a chance.

Doctors are required to have a minimum one hundred hours of continuing education every four years in order to keep up with the changes in their profession. If they're board certified, the requirements are much greater and include regular mandatory testing. Nurses are required to renew their licenses every two years with thirty hours of continuing education. As a new CPA in my home state of California, you must complete twenty hours of continuing education for each full six-month period from the date your license was issued to the license expiration date. After that, you must complete eighty hours of continuing education every two years. As an attorney in California, you are required to complete twenty-five hours of continuing education every three years.

And while some sales professionals have minimal standards of continuing education in order to remain up-to-date with the changes in their industry, to do away with the fatal mistake of stagnating once and for all, you must employ a regular continuing education plan that educates you on your industry's changes, and you must implement a plan that educates you on the changes in your life and keeps you at least one step ahead of your competition. At the end of every selling day, what will determine whether people are singing your dirge or your praises is the way you've stacked up against your competition. And whether you are one step or fifty steps ahead, the important thing is that you remain on the forefront.

But be careful. Your greatest competition is not out there somewhere. Your greatest competition is in the mirror. *Your greatest competition is yourself.* And when it comes down to it, if you can learn to continually be better than yourself—despite the mistakes you've made in the past—it won't be long before your clients will be singing your praises and clamoring for your business. It probably won't be long before *I'll* be singing your praises in another book. And I promise . . . I won't charge you a thing for the advertising. That's because it's always a pleasure to pass along the word about a first-class salesperson who knows what principles to apply—and to avoid—in order to run a first-class sales business.

Notes

Introduction

1. Statistics provided by the U.S. Patent and Trademark Office Web site <www.uspto.gov> as of May 2003.
2. Statistics according to the World Federation of Direct Selling Associations <www.wfdsa.org> as of May 2003.
3. Story from an anonymous contributor to the Monster.com Web-based archive titled *The Accidental Salesperson*.
4. Ibid.

Chapter 1

1. If you're interested in reading more about ascertaining your core motives, see my book *Life by Design* (J. Countryman, 2004) or Rick Warren's *The Purpose-Driven Life* (Zondervan, 2002) .

Chapter 2

1. My client's name has been changed to respect his privacy.

Chapter 3

1. "2 Paths of Bayer Drug in 80's: Riskier One Steered Overseas," Walt Bogdanich and Eric Koli, *New York Times*, May 22, 2003.
2. For a thorough discussion of the ingredients of a successful sale, see *High Trust Selling* (Thomas Nelson, 2002).

CHAPTER 4

1. Marilyn Irwin, a Verizon service representative from Maryland, as quoted by Loren Stein, a Consumer Health Interactive© medical advisor for Blue Cross Blue Shield of Minnesota <http://blueprint.bluecrossmn.com>, 5 December 2002.

2. As reported on August 18, 2000, in an article entitled "Forced Overtime and Job Security Issues in Verizon Strike" by an anonymous contributor to the World Socialist Web Site at www.wsws.org.

3. As reported in the September 2000 issue of *Broadband Week* by Karen Brown in her article titled, "Verizon Strike May Thump CLEC Third Quarter."

4. Report from an article titled "Forced Overtime" on the Blue Cross of Minnesota Web site <http://blueprint.bluecrossmn.com>.

5. Ibid.

6. Bryan Robinson, Ph.D., "The Workaholic Family: A Clinical Perspective," *American Journal of Family Therapy*, vol. 26, no. 1 (January–March 1998) 63–73.

7. See the full article by Karen Johnson titled, "The Trade-Off," at www.poppolitics.com.

8. Ian has increased his sales from $66 million/year to $100 million/year since the publication of *High Trust Selling*.

9. Tom has increased his sales orders from 200/month to 300/month since the publication of *High Trust Selling*.

CHAPTER 5

1. See the full write-up entitled "Overtraining" at www.intense-workout.com.

2. Many of these stories are detailed in *High Trust Selling*.

3. For relevant, top-notch coaching, contact Building Champions at www.buildingchampions.com.

4. Averages are based on clients who worked at least 40 hours per week and 50 weeks per year.

5. On pages 106–9 of *High Trust Selling* I teach how to master the skill of "Time-Blocking." See this section if you want further instruction on this discipline.

6. I highly recommend the experts at Building Champions <www.buildingchampions.com> for top-notch coaching advice.

CHAPTER 6

1. See complete poll results at www.gallup.com.

2. Story from an anonymous contributor to the Monster.com Web-based archive titled *The Accidental Salesperson*.

3. Dr. Theodore Zeldin is a former dean of St. Anthony's College at Oxford. He is quoted in an online article by SellingPower.com contributor Heather Baldwin titled, "The Art of Conversation."

4. The National Business Association is a 36,000-member small-business advocacy organization based in Dallas, Texas.

5. See complete poll results at www.gallup.com.

6. Dr. William Isaacs is the president of Dialogos, a consulting and leadership education firm based in Cambridge, Massachusetts. He is quoted in an online article by SellingPower.com contributor Heather Baldwin titled "The Art of Conversation."

CHAPTER 7

1. Probability percentage is based on the ratio of 1:24, or 1 sale made every 24 phone calls.

2. The National Consumers League is based in Washington, D.C. A full report on sales fraud in the U.S. can be found online at www.nclnet.org.

3. Joanna L. Krotz runs Muse2Muse Productions, a content strategy and editorial services firm. She is the founding editor of MoneyMinded.com, a women's money management site. Her full article can be found at www.bcentral.com.

Chapter 8
1. Story from an anonymous contributor to the Monster.com Web-based archive titled *The Accidental Salesperson*.

Chapter 10
1. As reported by a SellingPower.com electronic newsletter, 16 June 2003.
2. As described on page 33 of the book *Differentiate or Die* by Jack Trout and Steve Rivkin (John Wiley & Sons, 2000).
3. Trout and Rivkin, 7.
4. Magee, David, *Turnaround: How Carlos Ghosn Saved Nissan* (Harper Collins, 2003).
5. Ibid, 91–92.
6. Cook, John, compiler, *Book of Positive Quotations* (Minneapolis, Minn.: 1993).

About the Author

Todd Duncan is one of America's leading experts in the area of Sales and Life Mastery. His publisher, Thomas Nelson, calls him "an exciting combination of Zig Ziglar's energy and style, with John Maxwell's content."

Dr. John C. Maxwell says, "Todd just plain delivers the goods . . . and people's personal and financial lives are being tremendously and greatly impacted."

Todd Duncan has devoted the last twenty-three years to researching high-performance, successful people in all walks of business and life. His findings have been synthesized into one of the most powerful programs ever created on how to live a more meaningful, fulfilling, enriching, and profitable life.

Zig Ziglar says, "I know a little something about selling and success . . . and about motivating people to reach their goals. As I've watched Todd Duncan over the years, I've seen in him a lot of the same passion, the same spark, the same drive that has motivated me."

Todd's best-selling books and seminars have influenced millions of people. Of Todd's book *High Trust Selling*, Ken Blanchard says, "If you're serious about selling you must read this book. It's a breakthrough!" *High Trust Selling*, published by Thomas Nelson, is a *Wall Street Journal, Business Week, Los Angeles Times* and Barnes and Noble business best-selling book.

The Duncan Group has its corporate office in Atlanta, Georgia. Todd and his wife, Sheryl, have two sons and live in La Jolla, California.

www.theduncangroup.com

Acknowledgments

I'd like to say thank you to Sheryl Duncan, who inspires me to be all I can be, daily.

To Jonathan and Matthew Duncan, my sons, who are two of the greatest salesmen in the world

To Brent Cole, who does my writing.

To Amy Dickens, who makes my life so much easier.

To Victor Oliver, who shaped the idea for this book.

And to the people who are adding value to my life, enabling me to write books: Dennis Worden, David Childers, Daniel Harkavy, John Maxwell, Zig Ziglar, and the entire Duncan Group Team.

Where Do You Spend Your Time?

The answer may shock you. In fact, as much as 75 percent of the time you spend at work is probably *a waste of time*. That's right. 75 percent! If you're looking to the exploding field of time-management tools for answers, you're only wasting more time. After all, you can't manage time. The only thing you can truly manage is what you do with your time.

NEW YORK TIMES BESTSELLER
TODD DUNCAN
AUTHOR OF *HIGH TRUST SELLING*

TIME
TRAPS

PROVEN STRATEGIES FOR
SWAMPED PROFESSIONALS

If you're ready to propel your career and your life to new heights, *Time Traps* is the book. And now is the time.

ISBN: 0-7852-8833-3

How do you differentiate yourself from your fellow salespeople? Catch the sale they let get away!

WHO STOLE MY SALE?

23 WAYS TO CLOSE THE DEAL

TODD DUNCAN

New York Times best-selling author and sales expert Todd Duncan shares true stories from a variety of industries about how "next level" salespeople made the sale, closed the deal, kept their clients for the long term, and catapulted their own careers. Let this educational and motivational book do the same for you.

ISBN: 1-4041-0409-7